Sarah Schoonmaker Baker

The Children on the Plains

A Story of Travel and Adventure from the Missouri to the Rocky

Mountains

Sarah Schoonmaker Baker

The Children on the Plains
A Story of Travel and Adventure from the Missouri to the Rocky Mountains

ISBN/EAN: 9783337178109

Printed in Europe, USA, Canada, Australia, Japan

Cover: Foto ©Andreas Hilbeck / pixelio.de

More available books at **www.hansebooks.com**

THE CHILDREN ON THE PLAINS

A STORY OF TRAVEL AND ADVENTURE

FROM THE

Missouri to the Rocky Mountains.

LONDON:
T. NELSON AND SONS, PATERNOSTER ROW;
EDINBURGH; AND NEW YORK.
1871.

CONTENTS

		Page
I. The Decision,		7
II. The Young Travellers,		12
III. The Trader,		18
IV. A Petition,		29
V. In Camp,		36
VI. Sunday,		44
VII. Fort Kearney,		50
VIII. The Crossing,		56
IX. The Doctress,		64
X. A Fresh Start		76
XI. "This Philistine,"		80
XII. Port Laramie,		84
XIII. Mrs. Nutten,		96
XIV. Westward,		103
XV. Salt Lake City,		107
XVI. Realities,		113
XVII. Home,		116
XVIII. Conclusion.		119

THE CHILDREN ON THE PLAINS.

I.

The Decision.

The morning light was stealing gently over the "Great Plains," between the Missouri River and the Rocky Mountains.

In the midst of the wide prairie a company of emigrants had pitched their camp. Their white waggons had clustered there, like a flock of huge birds, the evening before, and now in the grey dawn the travellers were already astir. The smoke of their breakfast fires was slowly curling upward, and the only half-rested animals were being harnessed anew to the strong waggons. There was no spirit of cheerfulness and energy abroad in the camp. On all sides there were murmurings and bitter expressions of disappointment.

A few weeks before that same company had

started from Ohio full of eagerness and hope. On a May morning they had commenced their overland journey to California, with hearts as bright as the pleasant sunshine around them. Their white waggons were new then, and their horses were strong with the strength that comes from good care and proper food. Now the waggons were brown with the dust of their long journey, the poor beasts were tired out, and the emigrants had lost all their hope and courage.

One after another among them had been stricken with cholera, and they had dotted the road along which they had passed with the fresh graves of their companions.

When fairly on the plains their difficulties had daily increased, and the fatal disease seemed gaining ground among them. That night they had come to a decision. It was but five days since they passed Fort Leavenworth; they would go no further into the wilderness. They would turn back to the States, and exchange their golden dreams of California for hard work once more and a home of tolerable comfort.

There was not a dissenting voice in the whole company when the return was proposed, yet all were dissatisfied,—all were disappointed.

Every face was scowling with discontent, and not a little harsh language rose on the still air of that early morning We have said every face, but we must except two young countenances, of which we shall presently know more.

While stout men and sturdy women were busy about most of the waggons, round one two children were occupied.

Curtis Sumner, a boy of thirteen, was harnessing four mules for the journey, while his sister Ruth was carrying out his orders in the inner arrangement of the great vehicle.

Curtis and Ruth were favourites in the company; partly because they were the only children among the emigrants, and partly because they had been left motherless a week before, and so seemed to have a peculiar claim upon their fellow-travellers.

It had been a grievous trial to Ruth to leave the way-side grave where her mother was laid; but she had that sainted mother's parting command to fulfil, and this thought had given her resolution to go forward on her fatiguing journey. "Tell your father I hope to meet him in heaven," the dying wife had said; and Ruth believed in her heart that her erring father in California would hear this message, and take home its lesson to the good of his soul. On this thought the little girl had dwelt as Curtis wiped away her tears, and promised to be the best of brothers to her, now that she was left for the present wholly to his care.

The manly spirit of the boy, and Ruth's gentle quiet ways had daily won upon the emigrants, and there were many now to offer to assist them in their preparations, and to talk encouragingly to them of "going home again."

"We have no home now," Ruth was about to say; but she was silent, as she thought of the "happy home" her mother was already enjoying, and where she hoped, some day, to be welcomed. She would bear all present trials cheerfully, always keeping that home in view, and so she would never be desolate.

The preparations for departure were all made. The line of waggons stretched along the road, and but one more remained to close the gloomy procession. "Come, Curtis, follow up!" cried a hoarse voice from one of the vehicles.

Curtis drove his mules on to the road, but turned their heads in a different direction from what was expected. "*We* are going on to California. *We* see no reason for turning back. Our father will be expecting us," said Curtis. The news passed on from waggon to waggon, and there was a general expression of surprise and disapproval.

A number of the emigrants clustered about Curtis, and strove to dissuade him from his rash undertaking.

The boy was firm. He had a bold, determined

spirit. He feared neither death nor danger, and he would not give up his undertaking. As for Ruth, arguments were wasted upon her. She had her mother's message to deliver, and she would rather have died on the spot than have given up the hope of the great good she fancied this message was to effect.

"Well, you are your own master, I suppose, and must have your own way," said the rough farmer, who had first spoken to Curtis. "You must take your own chance; but I feel for your sister here. I had rather see her safe back in the States. Here, dear, take my brandy bottle, and my medicine box too; and, dear, keep up a good heart, and may be you'll get across safe after all!"

The rough fellow thrust his gifts into the waggon, wrung Ruth's hand till it ached, and then, wiping tears from his eyes, even while he gave a disapproving look at Curtis, he turned away

The others followed his example. The long line of waggons moved slowly towards the east, —while westward, towards the wilderness, went Curtis and his sister. Their choice was made; they were alone on the "plains," with only God for their friend.

II.

The Young Travellers.

THERE was nothing romantic in the appearance of Curtis and Ruth Sumner, and their travelling equipage. Curtis was but a tall, frank-faced boy, clothed in a suit of coarse grey cloth, and handling the reins like one used to the office, and skilled in country occupations.

Ruth, in her brown dress, plaid shawl, and close gingham sun-bonnet, sat up at his side, looking like the child of a western farmer, as she was.

The waggon itself was a great lumbering vehicle, whose outward beauty was not increased by the chicken-coop attached to it behind, or by the various baskets that hung from its sides.

The four mules must not be forgotten in the description. The two leaders, Bob and Jerry, were a fine, sleek pair of animals, that looked strong and well-fed, even after the fatigues they had undergone. Of the other pair, not as much that is favourable can be said. Joe was full of years, full of brown callous spots, and was supposed to be as full of discretion. Indeed, he needed much of the latter quality to keep in order the undue vivacity, viciousness, and obstinacy of his companion John, a young, half-broken creature, who could not have been trusted in the company at all, but for the safeguard of the good behaviour of his three associates.

Curtis had an attachment to every individual of the team, and as he started them off at a good round pace, he called Ruth's attention to their various merits, as unconcernedly as if he and his sister were setting out for a pleasure drive on an Ohio turnpike.

Curtis did not feel quite as much at ease as he wished to appear, but he thought an off-hand way of talking the best means of keeping up Ruth's courage at this trying moment.

Curtis might have kept his remarks to himself, for all the advantage they were to Ruth. At that instant she was seeking a surer source of strength, and staying herself upon a better consolation.

It was a relief to the little girl to escape from the rough people with whom she had been so many days associated. Their coarse, profane language, and loud, boisterous ways, had been most unwelcome to her, particularly at a time when she peculiarly realized the presence of the God who hateth iniquity, and will not have his name dishonoured.

Now a sweet peace was stealing over her heart.

In the quiet of the early morning she could lift up her soul to God, and trust herself and her future entirely to him. The "Plains" they were crossing, the world through which they must pass — she dreaded neither, with God as her friend.

One look at Ruth had satisfied Curtis as to the way in which she was occupied, and he relapsed into silence.

Beside his mother's grave Curtis had breathed his first real prayer. The good seed that mother had faithfully sown, had not sprung to life until watered by the warm tears shed when she was no more. Curtis meant to be a Christian. He had really begun heartily, but he was a stranger to serious thought, and it was hard for him to keep to his new resolutions. He longed to feel as Ruth did, and wondered if he ever should.

"Ruth," he said, after a moment's pause, "suppose you should sing a hymn for us to start with."

Ruth's face brightened. Such a proposal from her brother was most welcome. Curtis had said nothing about his new and better wishes, but Ruth fancied he was touched as he had never been before, and now his request was hailed as still another indication of a new sympathy existing between them.

Ruth had a sweet, bird-like voice, and now it

sounded out over the wide prairie, as from her heart she sang,—

> "Children of the Heavenly King,
> As we journey, let us sing;
> Sing the Saviour's worthy praise,
> Wondrous in his works and ways."

Hymn after hymn Ruth poured forth, as the waggon moved steadily along; at length she paused for a moment, and was recalled from her sweet thoughts to a full sense of their present condition.

"Look," said Curtis; "they are all out of sight."

Curtis drew up the reins, and Ruth leaned forward and looked out on all sides of her. The returning emigrants were no longer to be seen. In every direction the wide prairie swept away, in great waves, like a ground-swell on the ocean. Not a tree nor a shrub, nor even a rock, rose to vary the far-reaching landscape. The beaten emigrant road, winding across the plain, was the only trace the foot of man had left in that wilderness.

A sudden feeling of loneliness and desolation came over Ruth, like a cloud.

At that moment a small object near the road attracted her attention. She motioned to Curtis to be silent. Across the track flitted a prairie-hen, followed by her little brood.

There was something so home-like in the look of the little family, that it gave Ruth a feeling of comfort and companionship. It had, too, for her a better message: it told of Him who keepeth his children under the " shadow of his wings," and is as mighty as he is loving to protect.

From that time every living creature that she saw by the wayside, every flower that caught her eye, were to Ruth indications of the presence of the great Creator. She felt that he was in the wilderness with her, and she was sustained.

Curtis and Ruth were not to lose the sound of human voices, even on those dreary plains. That day they met, first, a little company, with a sick man in a waggon, going slowly back to the States; then a large party of emigrants on the same homeward track,—pale, thin, and disheartened.

They had sad tales to tell of days passed without water, and dying companions bemoaning the hour that had tempted them to leave their homes.

"Turn back! turn back! turn back for your lives!" was the advice that the children heard from all whom they met.

Curtis looked at Ruth. There was quiet determination in her eye as she said calmly, " We will go on."

Curtis had a wilful obstinacy of purpose, which made him always unwilling to abandon anything he had undertaken, and now he was most anxious to go forward. Ruth, however, was looking pale and weary, and Curtis, for the first time, questioned as to whether he was doing right to expose her to the hardships from which strong men turned back affrighted.

"Mother expected to have gone through it all. Mother chose to take me with her. I have her message to give to father. We *must* go on." This was Ruth's only reply to Curtis's offer to join the returning company, and give up the undertaking altogether.

Four and five times that day waggons came from the west and passed on to the east, yet Curtis and his sister no more spoke of returning. Others might be discouraged and go back—their voice was still, "Forward!"

III.

The Trader.

"I think we must have travelled thirty miles to-day," said Ruth, as Curtis drew up beside a small stream at nightfall.

"You girls always make out big stories. I don't believe it is more than fifteen. John has pulled back as much as forward, and if it hadn't been for old Joe, I believe we should have stopped altogether—at least, until Bob and Jerry smelt the water. See how glad they are to get a drink!"

The little stream was as refreshing a sight to Curtis and Ruth as it seemed to be to the tired animals. After a good long draught of the clear water, Ruth prepared to get supper.

"This is an old camping-ground," said Curtis, looking about him as if he were saying something very wise, whereas he was uttering only a self-evident fact.

There were various articles of household furniture strewed about the spot, as well as gardening implements, bags of beans, and band-boxes. In the midst of the confusion was set up a cooking-stove, which some emigrant had found heavy freight for so long a journey, and had discarded by the way. There it stood, as well furnished with pots, pans, and pokers as if it had been in a farmer's kitchen.

Ruth laughed to see herself so provided for, and Curtis went to work to knock up a discarded chair for firewood. The chicken that Curtis had killed by the way Ruth had nicely picked as they rode along, and now it was soon stewing over the fire, while the children congratulated themselves on having found so good a camping-ground.

"Quite like a home it seems, doesn't it?" exclaimed Curtis, cheerily. The thought of home brought tears at once to Ruth's eyes. Home without mother seemed an impossible thing to her.

Curtis had no time to think of Ruth's tears, for at that moment the sound of wheels attracted his attention. Turning quickly, he saw a long train of waggons coming from the west along the emigrant road. Ruth dreaded the sight of human beings more than she did solitude. The company of the rough men of the emigrant parties was worse to her than any loneliness. She feared, too, their influence upon her brother, who was much too ready to use the odd language he heard.

Ruth hoped the waggons would pass on, and leave their little camp unnoticed; but it was soon evident that their leader had no such intention. A small, strongly-built man, in the loose dress of a hunter, rode at the head of the train. At a signal from him the whole procession stopped, and then arranged itself into a circle round the spot where the children were preparing their supper.

The waggons were chained together so closely as to form a strong protection against any enemies, and but one opening was left to the enclosure.

"Are you the 'Babes in the Wood?'" said the leader of the party, speaking to the children in English, but with a strong French accent.

"No, sir!" said Curtis, with an air of great dignity.

"Where are you bound?" continued the questioner, chucking Ruth familiarly under the chin.

"We are going to California, to meet our father. Our mother died a week ago on the way, and the company we were with got discouraged, and turned back," answered Ruth calmly, though her heart beat very fast, and the tears were in her eyes.

"And you mean to go on alone! Well, you have good pluck," said the man kindly. "Young Mister there had better look out though, or he'll have the stiffness taken out of him before he gets many days further on."

Curtis made no reply, but pretended to busy himself about the waggon.

Ruth was left in possession of the cooking-stove for her operations, the new-comers prefering to make a fire on the ground, after their own fashion.

When Ruth and Curtis had taken their supper in the waggon, Curtis began to walk about the enclosure, and to make the acquaintance of the men. He soon learned that the leader of the party was Monsieur Collot, a French trader, who was on his way to Missouri. The waggons were loaded with buffalo hides, which M. Collot would easily dispose of as soon as he got to the States.

With the arrangements of the waggons Curtis was particularly pleased. He said it seemed quite like a fort.

"Yes, and a strong one too," replied one of the men. "We were attacked by a party of Indians two nights ago, but we were *coralled* as you see, and we beat them back, and never lost a man, nor even an ox in the fight."

Curtis felt a little strangely at the thought of such enemies being so near at hand, and yet he half wished he might meet some of the savages, so strong was his boyish love of adventure.

While Curtis was learning all he could from the party, Ruth was sitting on the front seat of the waggon, peering out at the strange scene around her. Darkness was creeping slowly on, and already the figures round the fire had a wild, fantastic air in the dimness.

"What do you think of us?" said M. Collot's voice close in Ruth's ear.

She turned suddenly, and saw the stranger at her side.

"I was wondering to see these people all look so cheerful, and seem to know so well how to manage," replied Ruth, truthfully.

"They don't do things like the raw emigrants who turned back chicken-hearted, then?" said the trader, smiling. "They are old hands at the business; this is not their first time crossing the 'Plains.' Experience is the best teacher."

"That is just what mother used to say," said Ruth, looking into the stranger's face more trustfully than before.

"A pretty nice mother I guess she was," remarked M. Collot, with an approving glance at Ruth.

Ruth's tongue was set at liberty by this remark, and, with all the enthusiasm of her loving nature, she spoke of her mother's sweetness and patience, her industry and her piety. Such a picture as Ruth drew of their pleasant home in

Ohio, fairly made the wandering trader's mouth water for the pleasures he had never known.

Ruth was just in the midst of describing the honeysuckle by the pantry window, that grew almost as fast as Jack's bean in the story, when M. Collot interrupted her,—

"What made you leave such a sweet place, chicky? Why, if I ever get into such a safe harbour, I shall know when I am well off, and stay there."

"My father," said Ruth, colouring and hesitating,—"my father had gone to California, and we did not hear from him for a good while, and then he wrote for us to come to him. Mother said we ought to go, and she wanted to go, I am sure. She never shed a tear, though I cried when I went round the place the last time, and bade good-bye to everybody, even to the cows, and the pigs, and the ducks. We had sold them all. We brought the chickens with us—my 'banties' too. I never could eat them, they seem so like people. When I hear them in the coop, then I feel almost as if I were at home again."

"I'll tell you what you'd better do," said M. Collot. "What is your name?"

"Ruth—Ruth Sumner," was the quick reply.

"Well, Ruth Sumner, you had better turn right round, and go back among folks that know you. Your father has got wild-like out there, I daresay, and won't care much about having children round him. To my thinking, you had better give up, and turn back with us. I won't leave St. Louis till I see you well started for Ohio, or looked out for there, if you like it better."

Ruth's face was very grave as she answered: "Mother said if father wanted us, we must go to him; and besides, I think when he hears how mother died, with such a smile on her face, and the word she sent to him, he'll be a different man. O sir, I'd go through a great deal to see that day."

"You love your father, then?" said the trader, with surprise.

"Indeed I do! Why, if he was only a good Christian man, he'd be the best father in the world! I've heard mother say so often. She said we would not any of us be worth anything if God did not help us to do right."

"I am not worth much, then!" said M. Collot, laughing.

"Don't you pray to God?" asked Ruth, quickly.

"No, child!" was the short answer.

"Have you a Bible?" said Ruth, who began to have a vague feeling that she was talking with a heathen.

RUTH GIVING HER BIBLE TO THE TRADER.

Page 5.

"No!" said M. Collot, with another laugh.

"I will give you one," said Ruth, very seriously; "Curtis will let me read in his, and you shall have mine—here it is."

Ruth drew from her pocket a small Bible, well marked, where her Sunday-school lessons had been learned, or texts that had pleased her well.

"See, it has my name in it; but you need not mind that. Won't you read it every day? you may die on the Plains, as mother did."

"You are a queer child," said the trader, taking Ruth's offered gift. "What you say is true. The day may come when I shall be glad to be like your mother. May be I'll look into it now and then." The trader now turned away, and was soon one among the group, taking supper round the fire.

Ruth had new food for thought, a new subject for prayer.

As she looked up to the clear skies, where the stars were already twinkling, it seemed strange to her that any one could live in God's world, and not love him. Very earnestly she prayed for the trader and his rough companions.

While the glow of the fire still lighted the enclosure, Ruth saw the trader take the book from his pocket and glance curiously into it.

With this pleasant thought in her mind, Ruth went to the lower end of the waggon, dropped the curtain that shut in her small sleeping apartment, and lay down to rest. It was late before Curtis returned to the waggon. The stories of the hunters were full of interest to him, and then he wanted, too, to see the little camp arranged for the night. He waited until the horses and cattle of the trader were driven into the enclosure, and the entrance barred. Then, with the noisy cries of the animals in his ears, he lay down to sleep.

Curtis was almost disappointed when he woke in the morning, to find that the night had passed away so peacefully, when matters were in so good a condition for a defence against savages and wild beasts. Ruth's waking thoughts were far different. Her first act was an uplifting of a grateful heart to the God who had preserved her through the night, and to whose care she trusted herself for the coming day.

There was no unnecessary noise and disturbance in the breaking up of M. Collot's camp. The thing was done promptly and quietly, and before the sun was fairly up the waggons were ranged along the road, ready for departure.

"You had better lighten your load here, Curtis," said the trader, familiarly. "Throw out everything but your food, powder, medicine, and the few clothes you need; all the rest is trash, to be parted with sooner or later."

"We haven't much else," said Curtis; "and as to powder, that would be of no use to us, as we have no gun."

"Out with the books, every one, and that great heavy trunk there; what's in it?"

"Only our crockery. It is packed very nicely," said Ruth, deprecatingly.

"Leave it here with the cooking-stove," said M. Collot, in a tone of command. "I can't, somehow, see you young folks setting out, without lending you a helping hand." Ruth had to see Curtis and M. Collot lifting out the trunk of crockery, and putting it beside the stove in the wilderness. The books—her mother's "Pilgrim's Progress" and "Baxter's Saints' Rest"—no, she could not part with them and a few others,—the sweet memorials of her mother's devoted piety.

"Now then," said M. Collot, when the load had been lightened, "now, Curtis, I am going to make you a present. This rifle I found by the road; some poor fellow lost it on the river's bank, where he was going to swim across. Can you shoot, sir?"

"Let me try," said Curtis, eagerly.

The first shot met M. Collot's approval, though John testified his entire dissatisfaction at the proceeding, and would have carried Ruth off the premises but for old Joe's obstinate resistance.

"There, now, the mule is right—you ought to be moving. I never stood so long before, after all was ready for a start. Take the rifle, boy, and this powder and ball. They may stand you in good stead. Now, good-bye to you—good-bye, my chicky."

"Good-bye—please read the good book!" said Ruth. M. Collot took the little volume from his pocket, and waved it, as he mounted his horse, and rode away to head the long procession moving slowly down the road.

Ruth followed him with a prayer.

Wandering in the West there are hundreds of such men, who never pray, who never read the word of God. Heathen they are, in land professing Christianity. Is there no way of sending the Bible among them? Is there no one to tell them of the "pearl of great price?"

IV.

A Petition.

Curtis quite enjoyed being the head of his own little party. It was amusing to see how readily he had caught M. Collot's manner; and through all the day the quick sharp tones of the Frenchman were heard in his voice when speaking to the mules, and even in giving his orders to Ruth. Orders, we say, for Curtis assumed it as a self-evident fact, that, being two years older than Ruth, and moreover a boy, she was bound to obey him on all occasions. Ruth did not prove an unruly subject, and it was not Curtis's fault if she formed habits of idleness along the road.

"M. Collot says it is a good plan to carry all your money about you," said Curtis, thoughtfully; "he spoke of having gold pieces stitched into a belt round his waist, under his clothes. Could you make such a thing, Ruth?"

"I daresay I could," said Ruth, brightening.

"Take that stout pair of duck trousers of mine, and make the belt out of it," said Curtis, decidedly.

"Are they not too good to cut up?" Ruth modestly asked.

"We must not load ourselves with useless baggage. Everything must be turned to the best account," said Curtis, looking very wise. "Make the belt, Ruth. That is the girl's part of the business."

"Hadn't I better make two—one for you, and one for me?" again asked Ruth.

"Of course not!" replied Curtis.

Ruth said no more. She took out her great calico needle-book, and began her work at once. The mules were moving slowly over hilly ground, and the little seamstress got on very well, making light of various pricks with the needle, which dotted the belt with red spots, though she did not mention them.

Ruth had just finished the belt, when she exclaimed, suddenly—

"Curtis! Curtis! Look! Look across the plain to the north-west!"

"I see only a few trees," said Curtis, jumping up at her side.

"No; they move!" said Ruth, decidedly.

"Give me my rifle!" said Curtis, promptly. The rifle was at his side, and he took it up himself, though he seemed to prefer to give out the order.

Curtis had hardly loaded his rifle, before the indistinct objects in the distance had become plainly defined as human beings moving rapidly towards the solitary waggon.

"They are Indians—I am sure of that!" said Curtis excitedly.

Ruth felt her blood chill, but she calmed herself with the remembrance that her Saviour was beside her.

"Drive quietly on, Curtis; perhaps they will take no notice of us!" said Ruth.

"No such thing! I mean to shoot down the first man that comes within ten yards of us!"

"O Curtis, that would be murder. You are not sure they mean to harm us!" said Ruth. "Only wait and see what they will do!"

The half-dressed beings were certainly Indians. On they came, with a long, loping motion, half run and half walk, and were soon very near the waggon.

Curtis stood up, and pointed his rifle directly at the foremost of the party.

The savage did not flinch. He merely said calmly his only English word, "Friends!" and put out, at the same time, a paper, as if he wished it to be read.

Curtis told Ruth to take out a fishing-pole that was lying along the edge of the waggon. "Hold it out, Ruth, for him to put the paper on the end, while I keep my eye on him."

Ruth did as she was bid. The Indian understood her meaning, and placed the paper on the pole, and Ruth slowly drew it towards her.

It proved to be a petition, written by some traveller, begging all who passed through this part of the country to give something to the poor Indians, whose wood they were burning, and whose home they were invading.

Ruth read the paper aloud.

"Pshaw!" said Curtis impatiently.

But Ruth remonstrated. "I have heard my mother say we owed the Indians a great deal, and ought to be kind to them. She said we would not teach them to be Christians by using them unkindly."

"We have no provisions to spare," said Curtis decidedly.

The Indians meanwhile looked on as if understanding the nature of the discussion.

"I will give them my bantams," said Ruth. Her fears seemed to vanish with the kind thought, and Curtis was surprised to see her get down from the waggon, and go the chicken-coop in the rear. Unlocking it, she took out her white bantams, and carried them to the Indian, at whom Curtis's rifle was still aimed.

The pretty white creatures were received with a shout by the Indians, and a grunt of gratitude addressed to Ruth.

Ruth caressed her pets as she parted with them, and the men seemed to understand that she was giving them something precious to herself. They looked at Curtis with a slight frown, but on Ruth they cast most approving glances.

Ruth had had a deaf and dumb friend in Ohio, and she was familiar with the language of signs. She did not find it difficult to understand that the Indians were pleased with her, and that they wanted to know why she was not afraid of them like the boy.

Ruth stopped for a moment. Then she looked up into the clear sky, as if in prayer. Then she made the movement as if she would say, "The Great Spirit holds me in his arms like a little babe, and I am safe." To her surprise, they seemed to take her idea at once, and looked upon her with sudden respect.

Ruth's surprise would have been less if she had known how largely the Indians use the language of signs. They have interpreters among them who go everywhere communicating with all tribes by the simple use of signs.

Curtis lowered his rifle as he saw his sister thus fearlessly holding intercourse with the Red men of the West. He was not pleased with the part he was playing in the interview. He resolved to take a new stand himself, and play Major Bountiful.

Taking down a piece of bacon that hung from the side of the waggon, Curtis held it out to the leader of the party with a most gracious bow.

The savage seemed a little suspicious of this overture. He leaped forward, seized the offered gift, and then bounded away across the prairie, followed by his companions.

"Poor creatures!" said Ruth compassionately, as she perched up again at Curtis's side. "They are as harmless as the old Indians who used to bring round their baskets in Ohio."

"Yes, these chaps seem of a friendly tribe," said Curtis; "but, Ruth, you would do well not to risk yourself quite so freely among them. The next may be of another sort. You would not relish having your scalp taken off."

Ruth shuddered, but she answered, "I don't suppose it is as much matter as we think it *how* we die, Curtis, if we only trust ourselves to the Saviour. I wish these poor Indians knew and loved him as we do."

"As *you* do," said Curtis humbly. "I am but little better than they are, I fear."

"O Curtis, do not say so! You are trying to love him, I am sure," said Ruth warmly.

"Sometimes, Ruth; but I forget all about it when I get interested in anything else," was the reply.

"We need his protection so constantly here, that it will help to keep him in mind. Won't it, Curtis? That will be one good thing about this journey for us," said Ruth, and she looked into her brother's face with one of her sweet, winning smiles.

"It is good for me that I have you with me," said Curtis fondly. "You are so like mother."

"So like mother!" That was the greatest compliment Ruth had ever received in her life. She felt quite humbled by it, and could only pray in her heart that she might have grace to follow the example of that mother who was now giving glory to God her Saviour in the heavenly "mansion."

V.

In Camp.

TRAVELLERS crossing the Plains learn to rejoice at the sight of trees, not only for their welcome shade, but because they only grow on the banks of the streams.

For several days Curtis and Ruth had been passing through a beautiful region, where the rolling plains were varied by winding streams, edged by oak, elm, and walnut-trees. The thirsty mules had enjoyed the cool waters, and the children had become so accustomed to driving through the shallow rivers, that Ruth no longer held fast to the side of the waggon, and grew pale as they went down the sloping banks. The evening of the fifth day of the children's lonely journey was coming on.

"How fortunate that we are just at this pretty place, the very spot for a camp!" said Ruth, looking about her with pleasure.

"Don't cry till you get out of the woods; we have the river yet to cross," said Curtis. "Now for it!" and he urged the mules into the water.

The Big Vermillion at this spot is two hundred feet wide and three feet deep, and as the current is strong the crossing is no easy matter. Joe and Jerry held up their heads wildly, and John straightened himself back, as if determined not to try such an uncertain business, at least with the waggon behind him. John had to give in, however, for the other three mules were obedient to Curtis's voice and the touch of his whip.

After some plunging in the miry bottom they came safely across, and then Curtis was willing to join with Ruth in praising their camping-ground. Near a fine spring of water they unharnessed the mules, and began to make preparations for supper.

"I am about tired of salt meat," said Curtis. "I wish you hadn't given the bantams away, Ruth."

"We should not have had them now, at any rate," said Ruth, laughing. "You can't keep your cake and eat your cake. Come, I'll fry the ham, just as we used to have it at home, and that will be a variety."

While Ruth was going on with her cooking operations, Curtis was exploring the spot they had selected for the night's rest.

He soon came back with his eyes full of delight. "Why, the trees here," he exclaimed, "are as good as the 'books' at a hotel, to tell who has been stopping here; and whose name do you think I have found?"

"Not father's!" exclaimed Ruth eagerly.

"Yes, father's—cut in an oak-tree, just as plain as can be. Come and see it."

There was the inscription, "Thomas Sumner, 1846, bound for California, famously well, in good spirits, but tired of salt meat!"

"That's father, exactly—full of fun," said Curtis, passing his knife along the letters, and freshening some that were becoming indistinct. "Here, we'll put ours just below, and say,— what shall I say for the benefit of those that come after?"

"Say, that by the kind care of our heavenly Father, we are still safe and well," said Ruth, gravely.

"Yes," said Curtis. "How is it, Ruth, that you always think such good things?"

"I don't always, Curtis. It is more mother's teaching than anything else, that makes me have such thoughts. Don't you remember when anything pleasant happened to her, how she was sure to say, 'Thanks to our heavenly Father?'"

Curtis had not finished his inscription, when the twilight made his work difficult, and Ruth called him to supper.

"I shall get up early to finish the carving. I must leave *our* names with the people's who have passed here. Why, there must be at least five thousand names here on the trees! I mean to tell exactly how old we are; that will make folks stare!" said Curtis.

Ruth thought it was of small importance whether "folks stared" or not, but she wisely refrained from saying so. Ruth kept out of many a quarrel by taking no notice of Curtis's foolish speeches, a lesson many a sister might learn to advantage. When Curtis awoke in the early morning he found Bob and Jerry enjoying themselves rolling on the grass, while Joe was quietly feeding. John, however, was performing some extraordinary gambols, which seemed more like movements of pain than pleasure, and so they proved.

All John's unwillingness to go in the right direction, and his fretting against his harness, had worked to his disadvantage. His back and neck were terribly galled, and it was plain that, for that day at least, he was not fit for use.

"We shall have to stop here to let John recruit," said Curtis, in his decided way.

"Couldn't you manage to tie him behind the waggon, and so not lose any time?" said Ruth.

If Curtis had thought of the plan himself he might have adopted it, but as it was he did not wish to take Ruth's suggestion; that would be an acknowledgment of inferiority for which he was not quite ready. Curtis, too, was a passionate lover of fishing, and he thought a day of rest, sitting under the trees, with his pole and line over the water, would be by no means disagreeable.

So it was decided that there was to be no moving on that day.

Ruth determined to do a great deal of mending, and to bake bread enough to last for three or four days at least.

This matter of bread-making was a slow process for Ruth, as she had but a Dutch oven, or bake-pan, to bake it in, and made it in small cakes, raised with soda and "cream of tartar."

She was more than half the morning busy around the fire; but when her labour was over, she called Curtis to see what a fine basket of bread she had laid in for their future use.

Curtis, meanwhile, had his treasures too to show. He had caught three large cat-fish, and a soft-shelled turtle; so the children had quite a feast, and grew as merry as if they were not alone in the wilderness.

Alone they took care to be, though hundreds of emigrants passed along the road that day.

As soon as it was decided that they were not to move on, they had changed their camping-ground to a more secluded spot, among the trees, where they would not be questioned by the various passers by.

These interviews with the emigrant trains were sore trials to Ruth, and she was glad to be one day off from the road, to escape them.

When all signs of the feast had been cleared away, Ruth took out her calico needle-book, and began to work at Curtis's coat, which needed mending.

"Won't you read to me, while I work?" she said, as she handed Curtis the Bible.

"If you wish it," said Curtis, with an unwilling yawn.

Curtis was in the midst of the story of Joseph, when he started up, saying, "I must take a little run on the prairie, Ruth; I am tired out, sitting here."

Ruth took the book from him with a sweet smile, and said, "Well, go then; I will sit here quietly till you come back."

Ruth was lost in some of the beautiful chapters of St. John, when Curtis came running up to her, with his cap in his hand.

"See! see!" he exclaimed. "Did you ever see finer wild strawberries than these?" The red, juicy fruit did look most tempting, and the brother and sister enjoyed them heartily together.

"I say, Ruth," broke forth Curtis,—"I say, I

believe I am very cross to you sometimes, and I don't mean to be. I love you dearly, and I want to be very good to you, but somehow, hateful things come in my mind to say. I was very angry when you asked me to read to you a while ago. Ruth, I don't love the Bible as you do, and I don't know what's to make me love it."

"You will have to ask God to help you, or you can never do what is right, or love what is good and true," said Ruth, gently. "Do you ever pray to him, Curtis?"

"Not exactly. To tell the truth, Ruth, when I go to pray, I can't think just what to say; and sometimes when I am trying to begin, my mind goes clear off, and I forget what I am about."

Ruth replied modestly: "I always say this prayer, every morning. It seems to ask for just what I want: 'Almighty God, who through thine only begotten Son, Jesus Christ, hast overcome death and opened unto us the gate of everlasting life, I humbly beseech thee, that as by thy special grace thou dost put into my mind good desires, so by thy continual help I may bring the same to good effect, through Jesus Christ our Lord, who liveth and reigneth with thee and the Holy Ghost, ever one God, world without end. Amen.' Mother taught me that prayer one day, when I said something to her like what you spoke of just now. Then there is the Lord's prayer, that says, you know, 'Lead us not into temptation, and deliver us from evil.'"

"Yes—yes," said Curtis, hesitatingly, as if still unsatisfied, or unconvinced of his duty.

"Suppose we pray together, every night and morning. Would you like that, Curtis?" said Ruth, in a low voice.

"I should," was the brother's only reply.

That night, when the stars began to twinkle in the sky, Ruth and Curtis knelt, side by side, under the lofty trees; and while Ruth raised her voice in prayer, Curtis strove to join her in his heart.

VI.

Sunday.

Curtis was waked the next morning by hearing Ruth singing, "Welcome, sweet day of rest," in her own cheerful way.

"Why, it is Sunday, I declare!" said Curtis to himself. The thought was not a pleasant one to him, for he had made up his mind to go on, whether John was able to bear the harness or not.

"Ruth," was Curtis's morning salutation, "I think we had better go on to-day. We took one day of rest yesterday. It really makes very little difference whether we sit here under the trees, or sit in the waggon; we can be as Sundayish when we are moving as when we are at rest."

"I am sure you are not in earnest," said Ruth anxiously. "You know what mother thought about keeping holy the Sabbath-day."

"I really don't see any difference. You can read to me, if you like, along the road; and we can't go to church anyway, so where's the odds?"

"We are commanded to let the cattle rest on the Sabbath-day," said Ruth. "It would not be resting for the poor mules to be dragging along to-day just as usual."

"The *poor* mules, indeed! Look at them now," said Curtis, laughing.

The mules were evidently enjoying themselves to their heart's content. Even Old Joe was rolling away on the grass, then indulging himself in some bounds that must have reminded him of the days of his youth. John looked on enviously, but did not seem in a mood to join his companions in their merry-making.

"John, at least, needs another day's rest," urged Ruth.

"Pshaw!" was Curtis's reply.

"Brother," said Ruth decidedly, "you are older and stronger than I am, and wiser in many ways. In most things I think it right to yield to you, but now I *must* have my way. I should not dare to be here, in the midst of so many dangers, if I did not trust in the God who watches over all who love him and try to serve him. How could I expect him to watch over me, if I were breaking one of his commandments? Brother, I will not go on to-day. I am sure you will not go and leave me here alone.

"Of course not!" said Curtis crossly.

This was not a pleasant beginning for Sunday

morning. This was a sad contrast with the joint prayer of the evening before, which had sent such peace into Ruth's heart. Curtis had little to say to Ruth through the morning. He wandered about picking strawberries, or casting envious eyes at the trains of travellers which passed along the distant road.

Ruth, meanwhile, had her own Sunday joy. She knew that she had done her duty, and she felt sure that the loving eye of God was upon her.

She had her dear little prayer-book with her; and as she knelt under the tall trees in that lonely spot, it was joy to her to know that she was speaking the same prayers that were going heavenward from many true Christian hearts at that very time.

Her simple hymns she was sure would be as welcome to the heavenly King as if she were joining in the singing of the "great congregation."

Ruth's Bible was full of comfort to her that day, and as she read of the New Jerusalem, she fancied she could feel some of the joy of that glad home, where tears shall be for ever wiped away.

Ruth was too happy to mind Curtis' sullen looks when he came at mid-day to share the simple repast prepared for him.

"How pleasant it is that the sun is under a cloud just now," said Ruth cheerily.

"A cloud that's likely to give us a wetting," said Curtis, looking anxiously about him. "We must take shelter in the waggon."

The storm rose very fast. The black clouds rolled up the sky, like smoke before the breeze. The distant thunder muttered, then came nearer and nearer, while the incessant lightning glared fearfully over the landscape. The wind broke suddenly on the stillness. A fierce, wild hurricane it proved, sweeping all before it. Tall trees bent, bowed, and were cracked asunder. The rain poured in torrents.

"Cover yourself up, Ruthy; you will be wet through," said Curtis kindly. He gave his sister his blankets, and then he peered out from front of the waggon.

Curtis had never before known what it was to suffer agonizing fear. Now he seemed to himself to stand in the presence of an offended God. What would become of his soul if it were suddenly called into the presence of its Maker! This thought filled him with terror.

Even as he asked himself this question the lightning streamed down from the skies, and filled the whole air with electric light. The thunder roared with deafening peals.

A tall tree, at a little distance from the waggon, was splintered from top to root. Under that tree the affrighted mules had taken refuge. One of them dropped dead upon the spot. Yes, immovable—stiff in death he lay, while the torrents of rain poured down upon him.

Curtis was awe-struck. Such might have been his fate but for the mercy of God.

Curtis had been softened, touched, moved to better things at his mother's grave, but death had not even then seemed so near to him as it did in the midst of that fearful storm.

Ruth was lying in the waggon, very quiet, in the midst of the wild uproar. She felt herself safe in the hands of Him who " ruleth the heavens," and "taketh up the isles as a very little thing."

" Ruth!" said Curtis; " Ruth, are you frightened?"

"God is with us. If we trust in him, we cannot be harmed," replied Ruth solemnly.

"But we may be killed. That last flash struck down poor old Joe! It might have been one of us," said Curtis quickly.

" Death cannot harm us if we trust in Christ," was Ruth's reply.

Curtis was silent. Ah! how he felt his *need of Christ* at that moment! How was he, a poor sinful boy, to stand before God, unless forgiven for Christ's sake? He felt the full meaning of a Saviour, a Redeemer, then!

To that Saviour he fled for refuge, as to his only hope.

The storm was passing by, even while the earnest prayer to God for forgiveness and an humble, penitent spirit, was rising from the heart of the conscience-stricken boy. Swiftly as the clouds had gathered they sped away, and the sunshine again made glad the landscape.

Curtis and Ruth were thoroughly drenched in spite of the precautions they had taken.

"It is well we are not on the prairie, where we could get no wood," said Curtis, as he with difficulty kindled a fire with some fallen timber and broken branches.

A great roaring fire was at length made, and near it, and in the pleasant sunshine, Ruth and Curtis hung up their valuables to dry.

"I shall never forget this Sunday," said Curtis very gravely when they were once more comfortable, and the sun was setting clear in the west. "I shall never forget this Sunday. I shall never ask you to break the Lord's day again, Ruth."

VII.

Fort Kearney.

More than two weeks had passed since the Sunday in camp, described in the last chapter.

For four days the children had been travelling along the banks of the Little Blue river, and now the road turned away from it, and the landscape, without water, seemed dull and dreary.

"I am quite attached to the little river; I can't bear to leave it," said Ruth to Curtis.

"And so am I. It seems like company," said Curtis, with a lingering look at the bright water.

Ruth held in her hand a bouquet she had gathered. Strange-looking flowers they were, such as she had never seen before. There was a bright purple lupine (the blossom of which grows directly from the root, "without a leaf at all"), a blue digitalis, and a mallow of such a beautiful deep pink, that Curtis said it was just the colour he should like to see on Ruth's cheeks.

Those same cheeks would have been very

pale, but for the clear, brown tan that gave them a healthy hue. Poor Ruth was getting tired out. For six weeks she had been on this fatiguing journey, bearing all annoyances with cheerfulness, but daily losing strength and vigour.

Curtis, meanwhile, seemed to have profited by the life of exposure he had been leading. Ruth declared he had grown more than an inch since he left Ohio. He did look very tall for a lad of thirteen; perhaps he had straightened himself up since he had had the responsible position of chief of his little party.

Curtis and Ruth had been chatting along for mile after mile, when at last the mules slowly ascended a sandy ridge, across which the road led.

Curtis drew up the reins suddenly at the top of the ridge.

"Look! Look, Ruth!" he exclaimed.

The scene was well worth a careful survey.

Through the broad green valley that lay before them flowed a wide river, with a long island stretching along its midst—an island covered with tall trees more than a century old.

"This must be the Platte!" said Curtis, in a knowing way.

"The Platte river!" exclaimed Ruth, in delight. "Why, I've learned about it in my

'Geography.' I've seen it on my map! Let me think. 'The Platte rises in the Rocky Mountains, has a general easterly course, and flows into the Missouri.' That is the way we used to *describe* it at school."

The sight of the Platte was very cheering to the children. It seemed like being in known regions to see a river that was on the maps, and talked about even by little children in Ohio.

"It must be the Platte. See how shallow it is, and how restless and muddy, just like the Missouri! That's what M. Collot said. He told me we would certainly know it when we came to it, and then we should be within a day's journey of Fort Kearney. Take heart, Ruth; we shall see houses before night."

Almost as welcome to Ruth was the idea of seeing human dwellings as is the sight of the green shore to the sailor who has lately been exposed to a wild storm on the ocean. The thought of rest made Ruth realize how tired she was, and how glad she should be to be settled and quiet in a home once more.

Ruth did not say one word about these feelings, but Curtis guessed them. He rolled the flour barrel forward in the waggon, so as to make a back for Ruth's seat, and threw a doubled blanket over it, to make it soft for her to lean against.

Curtis was growing more and more fond of his little sister, and watchful for her comfort. Ruth's sweet, uncomplaining spirit was having its daily influence upon her brother.

The mules travelled but slowly that day; John was very troublesome. Curtis had tried in vain to harness him so as to draw with Bob and Jerry. John seemed to have a notion that old Joe was somewhere at play, and that it was an imposition to try to make a younger animal still keep at work.

Curtis had given up trying to use John for draught, and had loaded him with some articles to lighten the weight of the waggon, and tied him behind it. Being thus limited in his prospect, and uncertain where he was going, John was in a continual state of mutiny, and Ruth had to spend a good deal of her time looking through a little opening in the rear of the waggon, and talking to the contrary creature to coax him along.

Curtis had found a scythe, dropped by some overloaded emigrant, and now when he came to a patch of tall grass, he cut it down, and stored it in the waggon.

This good cheer Ruth doled out to John in small handfuls through the loophole, and so, by coaxing and feeding, the odd creature was induced, for a part of the time, not to pull back while the other mules were pulling forward.

At the close of the day's journey Ruth was neither leaning against the flour barrel, nor administering to John's obstinacy. She was fast asleep in her own little apartment at the end of the waggon. She, poor child, was fairly tired out.

She started up suddenly from her sleep in a wild fright. Where could she be? What could be the matter? The sound of martial music was in her ears.

"What is it? What is it, Curtis?" she exclaimed.

"Come out here and see!" was Curtis's cheerful reply.

Ruth peered out from the front of the waggon, and a welcome sight met her eyes. They had reached Fort Kearney! There were the long, low buildings with flat roofs, all built of adobe, or sun-dried bricks. There were tents upon tents,—tents for workshops and for soldiers, for sick men and for officers. Quite a village, indeed, in its own way.

Very kind was the reception the tired children met with at Fort Kearney. A kind-hearted officer gave up to Ruth his own bedroom, and such sweet sleep as she had was better than any cordial to her weary limbs.

Curtis had a supper that made him forget all about salt meat,—a supper of buffalo beef, rich and juicy, the very choice part of the whole great animal.

Curtis and Ruth stopped a whole day at Fort Kearney. Their waggon needed mending, Curtis said, and one of the soldiers had promised to show him how to load a pack mule, and to bring John into better subjection. Curtis did not say that Ruth looked weak and weary, but the fact had as much influence in inducing him to put off starting as the wants of the waggon or of John.

Ruth had a real heart-warming in one way at Fort Kearney. The officer who had provided for her so kindly had talked to her gently and pleasantly, not like the rough, coarse men she had met on the emigrant road. He had told her of his own little girl, the same age as herself, whom he had left at home in the East. But this was not all; he had spoken to her of the heavenly Father! He was a true follower of the Lord Jesus, and was trying there in the wilderness, among rude soldiers and still ruder savages, to spread abroad the spirit of the gospel of peace.

VIII.

The Crossing.

When Ruth bade good-bye to her friend, the officer, and looked her last upon Fort Kearney, she felt as if she were leaving a kind of home, or rather an oasis in the desert she was crossing. A green spot in memory, she was sure, her stay at Fort Kearney would ever be. Something of this sort she said to the kind-hearted officer, who shook her hand affectionately as she jumped into the waggon,—something having the same meaning, though not the same words.

His deep "God bless you, child; I believe we shall meet again in the better country!" was his only reply.

Curtis shook the reins, and the great waggon was again in motion. More than three hundred miles the children had travelled since they left Fort Leavenworth, and yet they were but little more than at the beginning of their journey when they turned from Fort Kearney. Along the banks of the Platte the children journeyed —journeyed for two whole weeks.

At night they often drove through the shallow

waters to some island near at hand, to encamp under the trees, and to let the mules enjoy the rich grass.

Trees, shrubs, and often even grass, seemed to have been burned away along the valley, while in the islands alone vegetation was flourishing.

Many buffalo paths the children had seen, deeply worn into the ground by the heavy feet of the great animals, but not a single buffalo had yet crossed their track. Curtis talked bravely of his anxiety to fall in with a herd of these animals, and try his rifle upon them; but Ruth ate her bacon and bread, and was thankful to be safe from dangers such as she fancied they would risk among a herd of buffaloes on the Plains.

Some smaller animals the children saw which interested them not a little. They came upon a regular settlement of prairie dogs. Each little creature had his own hole or home, and there he stayed, with his head out, barking at the children as if he were not pleased at their driving through his village without paying toll.

Through the barking settlement Curtis drove slowly, watching the animals with interest, until John became almost frantic, fancying, possibly, that he would presently have the whole crew about his heels.

"I'll kill one of the little scamps, and make

an example of him!" said Curtis, pointing his ever-loaded rifle at one of the dogs.

Before Ruth could speak the ball had done its work, and the little creature dropped back dead into the recesses of its under-ground home.

"I'll pull him out—I want to have a look at him," said Curtis, springing from the waggon and thrusting his arm into the hole where the prairie dog had disappeared.

A quick, sharp rattle caught Curtis's ear. Ruth, too, heard the sound. They both knew it well. They had twice heard it in Ohio. "A rattle-snake! A rattle-snake! O Curtis!" exclaimed Ruth in terror.

Curtis was at her side in a moment unharmed.

"O brother! I was so frightened! How thankful we ought to be!" she exclaimed.

"I believe I am," said Curtis gravely. "That was a narrow escape."

"What a mercy it is that the horrible thing rattles before he strikes. It seems like a warning sent by our heavenly Father to save us from harm," said Ruth earnestly.

"I shall remember again what I hear," said Curtis. "I wish I could always think before I move. One of the soldiers at Fort Kearney told me about the prairie dogs, but I thought he was making game of me. He said there was generally a rattlesnake in every hole, and an owl too!"

"How strange!" said Ruth, laughing. "Such a queer company! It does not seem as if it could be true!"

Curtis was very fond of natural history, and not at all unwilling to let Ruth see how much he knew. He was eagerly discoursing on the habits of the owl, when they came to the spot where the road crosses the south fork of the Platte.

"Here we are at the ford!" exclaimed Curtis. "The river is pretty full. I think I'll send John over first and see how he makes it out."

Curtis put John's load into the waggon, and then forced the animal into the water. John did not like the look of the stream; it was half a mile wide, and thick with yellow mud. However, he determined at last to make the best of it, and plunged in.

Curtis watched him carefully, until he at last reached the opposite bank.

"He had footing all the way, that was plain —so here we go!" said Curtis, as he urged Bob and Jerry forward.

"Going it bravely! eh, Ruth?" said Curtis triumphantly, when they were more than half way over.

At that moment the waggon came to a sudden standstill. Deep, deep into the mire it was plainly sinking. The mules pulled, and struggled, and jerked again and again, but all in vain. Not an inch did they advance. The waggon had plainly become a permanent fixture, fast to the river bottom.

"What was to be done?" This question Curtis and Ruth could not answer at once.

"If you could only swim, Ruth!" said Curtis, with a woeful look at his helpless sister.

"*Must* we give up the waggon?" said Ruth dolefully.

"I don't see any other way. We can't get it out! Bob and Jerry won't stand it long, pulling at this rate in the water, and the current is so strong. Do you think you could ride Jerry through the water if you were once on his back?"

"I would not be afraid to try," said Ruth, mustering up her courage.

"I'll loosen them from the waggon," said Curtis.

Ruth managed to get on Jerry's back, and Curtis soon took his place beside her on Bob. Ruth grew more and more courageous as they advanced. She saw all around swift-flowing waters, that might at any moment overwhelm her. Ruth did not like her position; but she saw it was no time for cowardice or complaining. She thought of Peter walking on the water to meet his Saviour, and into that

Saviour's keeping she put herself in that time of danger.

Once loosened from the waggon, the mules made their way quickly through the river, but with such an unsteady motion that Ruth had hard work to keep her seat, clinging as she was to Jerry's collar, and perched on his back without a saddle.

Both the children and the mules were thoroughly exhausted when they reached the shore in safety.

"I must rest a little, and then go back on Bob to save what I can from the waggon," said Curtis, after seeing Ruth safely seated on dry ground.

Curtis was able to make but a few trips to the waggon, before both Bob and Jerry utterly refused to enter the water again. The poor animals were much worn down by their long journey, and latterly had moved but slowly, even when the road was the best.

Curtis looked at Ruth despairingly: "I could manage it alone, but, Ruthy dear, I'm afraid you'll never be able to stand riding on Jerry, with such a saddle as I can contrive for you. See, we've got nothing now for the journey but my rifle, and powder, and ball, and my fishing-tackle. I was careful not to forget them. Here's the hatchet, too, and the blankets, and the extra harness. I meant to get the bacon next time. I believe I must make Bob go in again.

"Don't! Don't, Curtis! He might throw you. You know how he does when he's fairly out of patience!"

"Let him, then! I can swim. I won't be mastered by a mule,—especially when so much depends upon my having my own way," was the brother's obstinate reply.

"Dear Curtis, don't!" said Ruth pleadingly.

Curtis was mounting again, when a glance at Ruth's mournful countenance changed his mind. He felt that he had no right to risk his life, and run a chance of leaving his sister unprotected in the wilderness.

"Well, we must go on, I suppose, the best way we can," he said, somewhat sullenly.

He then strapped some blankets across Jerry's back, and when Ruth was fairly seated on them, he saddled Bob after the same fashion for himself. The few things that had been saved were placed upon the other mule. The doleful procession then started forward.

The day was more than half over, but without provisions, as they were, Curtis declared it was madness to stand still, waiting for something to come to them.

"The Lord will provide for us; I am willing to go on," said Ruth, cheerfully.

For several hours the children rode slowly forward in silence. Ruth did not complain of the fatigue that was almost overpowering her, but she could not talk.

"That must have been a camping-ground," said Curtis, pointing to a spot a little off from the road. "I see some dark objects scattered about there."

The mules were quickly guided to the place that had attracted the boy's observing eye.

The camping-grounds of the emigrants are not marked alone by the signs of fires, and the names carved upon the welcome trees. At such spots there is sure to be a strange collection of articles, abandoned by the discouraged and over-loaded emigrants. Even persons making pleasure-trips in thickly settled Europe, soon learn to carry as little luggage, and to have as few wants, as possible; but this is an absolutely necessary lesson for emigrants on the "Plains."

What had been abandoned as useless burdens proved real treasures to Ruth and Curtis, in their hour of need.

They actually found a hundred pounds of bacon, stacked there because it was too heavy to be carried any further; while two barrels of flour were placed close beside the bacon. As directly sent by Heaven these stores seemed to Ruth, as did the ravens with their welcome food to weary Elijah.

IX.

The Doctress.

The children's bedroom admitted too much light to render late morning sleep desirable. They had no curtained windows to favour lazy dozing, and as soon as the sun brightened up the eastern sky, they were awake and preparing for their journey.

They were both suffering sadly from thirst. Ruth's tongue was parched, and felt like paper; Curtis could not suppress his complaints, as he moistened his lips with the dew that beaded the grass.

"If we only had a camel!" said Curtis, as he laid an India-rubber water-bag among the articles with which John was to be loaded. "But this bag some poor fellow has left behind, and it must answer the purpose when we find good water."

The old camping-ground was carefully searched by the children, and everything that could be useful to them was packed upon John's back.

The little party set out, by no means in good spirits. Ruth was quiet; Curtis cross, and the mules jaded, and evidently failing in strength.

The emigrant trains usually so unwelcome a sight to Ruth, she now would gladly have welcomed, if but a single cup of cold water could have been obtained from them. For a wonder the road was perfectly deserted. Not a single white waggon varied the dull line of the seemingly interminable pathway.

The children rode on in silence, upward, upward, as they crossed the bluff which divides the waters of the South and North Forks of the Platte.

The crest of the ridge was reached at last, and weary as the children were, they could not help stopping to admire the beauty of the scene stretched out before them. On one side was the wide rolling prairie they had just crossed; on the other, a landscape varied by rocky ridges and deep ravines, which, as it seemed, only an experienced mountaineer could cross in safety.

Ruth, and even Curtis, soon had enough to do to keep their seats, as the mules toiled up and down the steep hills, there being scarcely a single level spot on all the road.

"It is well we haven't the waggon here. I don't believe we could have managed with it," said Ruth, who always saw a bright side in every difficulty.

"Sure enough!" said Curtis, quickly. "Bob and Jerry would not have stood the waggon's pushing upon them, as it would have done going down such hills as these, and we really have pretty nearly all we need, except water, and we can't go on long without that."

"God will not forsake us," said Ruth, earnestly and devoutly.

For a few moments they rode on in silence, and then Ruth suddenly exclaimed—

"Look! Look, Curtis! There's an antelope," and she pointed to the spot where the little creature stood watching their movements.

"I'll shoot him! The taste of fresh meat would do something towards quenching this terrible thirst."

Curtis dismounted as he spoke, and rifle in hand, he stealthily approached the prize. The watchful animal did not wait until Curtis was close at hand; he bounded away, to stop and gaze at his pursuer when fairly beyond his reach. So Curtis was led on, ever hoping to reach the little creature, and ever disappointed by its taking a fresh run, until he was at some distance from the road where he had left Ruth in charge of the mules. Here the antelope disappeared from view.

"This is too bad. It seems I am not to have even this relief!" said Curtis pettishly.

Even as he spoke a joyful sight caught his eyes. There, among the rocks, sparkled a spring of pure, fresh water,—such water as he had not seen since he left Missouri.

Curtis, when he tasted the reviving draught, felt rebuked for his want of trust, and even before he went to tell Ruth of the good news, he knelt to ask forgiveness from the watchful heavenly Friend who had thus provided for him in the midst of his complainings.

Ruth's pale face flushed with pleasure when she heard of the discovery that Curtis had made.

"That antelope was Heaven's guide sent to lead you to the spring, Curtis!" said Ruth.

"I believe it!" said Curtis, seriously. "I never mean to despair after this."

Thoroughly refreshed by the pure water, the little party again set out on their journey, taking care to fill the India-rubber bag with a supply of the best of beverages, to last for the remainder of the day.

Curtis and Ruth had nearly reached the North Fork of the Platte, when the road along which they were travelling suddenly swarmed with human beings. There could be no mistaking those wild, half-naked forms, and Ruth knew at once that they were Indians.

Curtis seized his rifle, but in vain. It was taken from him at the instant by a strong hand from behind, while a tall Indian at the same moment took his mule by the bridle.

In silence the whole party now turned off from the road, down the bed of a narrow stream, that was now dry.

Curtis looked at Ruth. Her face was very pale, but it was full of peace, and he strengthened his own heart with the thought of her faith.

After an hour's silent ride, the whole party stopped at an Indian village or encampment. Ruth and Curtis were left in charge of two tall Indians, while the rest of the party gathered about them—men, women, and children—as if for a general consultation.

Curtis's mind was full of vague images of torture and death, and he was trying to nerve himself to bear whatever might come like a hero. Ruth meanwhile allowed no visions of terror to agitate her mind. By a strong effort of faith she realized the presence of her Saviour, and was calmly awaiting the result of this singular adventure.

About forty white lodges, or huts made of buffalo skin, were scattered along the green bank of the river. Before each lodge were tall poles, on which were hung a white shield, a spear, and a buck-skin bag.

After much consultation among the Indians, Curtis and Ruth were separated.

Curtis struggled to be free, as he saw Ruth led away on foot towards the largest of the huts, before which hung a great shield ornamented with curiously-painted devices.

The boy's struggles were in vain. Two strong hands clasped him like a vice, while his two keepers stood immovable.

Full of silent prayer, Ruth was led from the glad daylight into the dusky atmosphere within the tent.

No instrument of torture, no savage cruelties awaited her there in that silent spot.

Stretched upon a rude bed lay a young Indian girl. Her long black hair was pushed back from her face, and her dark eyes gazed wildly and eagerly at the new comer.

Ruth returned a look full of wonder and pity.

The Indian girl was wrapped in buffalo robes, richly embroidered, and her scarlet leggings and soft moccasins were wrought in the same manner, with gaily-coloured porcupine quills.

Her dress declared her to be a person of importance. There was respect, too, in the manner in which she was approached by the two Indians who ushered Ruth into the lodge.

There was eager expectation in the face of the sick girl, as one of the Indians, in broken English, now told Ruth her story, which was in substance as follows:—

The chief of this band of Sioux or Dacotah

Indians was absent with a party of his braves. Meanwhile his young daughter had fallen sick with cholera. Full of alarm at the terrible disease, she at once believed death certain for her, and would have herself arrayed as if already dead, and laid out to await her burial. She affirmed that there was no hope for her but from the white men, who, she had heard, had cures for the awful malady. The Indians had been struck with a double cause of terror; they not only feared the disease itself, but the anger of the chief, her father, should he return and find his child in the grave.

In haste they had sought the emigrant road, hoping to find there some persons who would render them assistance. They brought back our little travellers, silently, and with speed.

The wiser among the Indians at once said that these children could do no good to the sufferer. Then an old Indian, more experienced than the others, gravely spoke, saying he well knew that the overwhelming fear that had taken possession of the chief's daughter was her greatest danger, and for this he thought they had secured a remedy. He at once went to the silent tent, where the poor young Indian girl was lying, and told her that a pale-faced child had come among them,—a wonderful child, who had more power than many "medicine-bags," and

RUTH PRAYING FOR ANOTAH.
Page 71.

that she could cure the cholera even if the patient were actually dying.

Hope rallied in the Indian girl's heart when she heard this news; and now she looked eagerly at Ruth, as if expecting at once the marvellous cure.

The broken English, on which the old Indian prided himself, was not understood by the chief's daughter. She had lain in silent expectation while Ruth listened to the strange story. "Now," said the Indian, "now, cure quick—make she think it, or—" and he shook the spear at his side, to indicate a dreadful threat.

Ruth would not, even in that hour of danger, act a part to impose upon the poor sufferer. At once she resolved what to do. Leaning over the sick girl, she looked tenderly into her face; then taking her hand, Ruth lifted her eyes to heaven and prayed aloud. For the recovery of the stricken girl she prayed, and for all her people she asked the blessing of God—even the knowledge of his Son, Jesus Christ.

That was no praying for effect. Ruth eagerly longed for that which she asked, and she believed that she should receive it for Christ's sake. The wild fright, that had been the worst enemy of the Indian girl, was calmed as she looked at Ruth's sweet, earnest face, and heard the clear, musical tones of her voice. She fancied that the Great Spirit had sent the young stranger to her relief, and hope sprang up in her heart.

Curtis was surprised and rejoiced to see Ruth come forth safe from the lodge, with an added expression of peace on her usually placid countenance.

"She do well! She good doctor!" said the old Indian, as he drew near to Curtis.

Curtis, who had all this time remained between his two guards, was forthwith ushered into one small white lodge, and Ruth into another, left entirely vacant for their use.

Though dogs, papooses, squaws, mules, and ponies were thronging round the entrances, none were allowed to come in. One mother actually dragged away her creeping, curious child by the heels, just as he had got his head in at an opening in the curtain to get a peep at Ruth.

Boiled buffalo meat, served up in an old tin pan, was given first to Curtis and then to Ruth. Buffalo skins were handed in to them, and the Indian interpreter then told them they might as well go to sleep and get rested, for they would not start away for that day at least, and perhaps not for many more.

Ruth was astonished to find herself established in the position of a wonderful doctress, and forced to make daily visits to the lodge of the chief's daughter, who was evidently recovering.

Ruth's charm was very simple. She did but pray earnestly for all the Indian tribes, sing hymns, and as the sick girl listened she grew better. There was, indeed, a charm in Ruth's loving voice and gentle manners, very soothing to the invalid.

This time of rest was just what Ruth needed; while Curtis was heartily enjoying the novel scene of the encampment and the wild adventures of his Indian associates. Mounted on a good horse, he went out with fifty of the Indians who were on a buffalo hunt, and when at evening they returned, laden with the most juicy portions of the slain animals, he enjoyed the good cheer almost as well as his savage companions. Curtis had always reckoned his appetite by no means delicate, but he was astonished at the enormous quantities of food consumed by the Sioux braves.

Indians seem to have the power of laying in, at favourable seasons, a quantity of food and strength for future hardships. A single Indian has been known to eat, at one sitting, as much food as five white men would need for a hearty meal.

Anotah, the chief's daughter, daily grew more fond of Ruth, and her dark eyes were sure to brighten whenever the pale-faced visitor entered the lodge. By means of the interpreter, Ruth was trying very hard to give Anotah a knowledge of the true God, an the child of the wilderness was ready to believe all her loving doctress told her.

Meanwhile the troops of mules, horses, and cattle, owned by the Indians, had been cropping close the grass, far, far around the village. The chief had returned, and had at once given orders for a removal to better pasturage.

Anotah came out of her lodge to welcome him. She made him thank, through the interpreter, the little "pale face" who had, she said, saved her from death.

The chief looked upon the young doctress with favour, as one who had performed a skilful trick; but by no means felt towards her the wonderful gratitude which had taken possession of Anotah.

The village was soon all confusion, as preparations were being made for a prompt removal.

Curtis was pleased to see Bob provided with a comfortable Indian saddle, on which he was desired to mount; but he was troubled to see Jerry used as a pack mule, and placed side by side with John. What was to become of Ruth?

Several strange-looking conveyances Curtis had seen made in the following manner:—Lodge-poles were fastened at each side of a horse, with the long ends trailing on the ground far behind the animal. On these trailing poles a kind of wicker basket was hastily woven, with curved sticks over it, like the frame of a covered waggon. A blanket thrown over the whole affair made a sheltered place in which the Indians carried their light valuables, their puppies, and their babies.

From such an odd vehicle Ruth put out her head to nod encouragingly to Curtis as she passed, and to say the motion of her carriage was by no means disagreeable. Anotah, who had been more frightened than ill, was now quite strong. She walked at Ruth's side, much amused to see the little fair face peeping now and then from among the Indian babies.

Dogs were made to carry burdens in the same way; and it amused Curtis to see them trotting along, with their baskets behind them, carrying their puppies safely, mile after mile, just as Ruth herself was riding.

For a week the Indians were travelling, making halts by the way to refresh themselves, but not fairly setting up their lodges until within three days' journey of Fort Laramie.

Ruth, meanwhile, was treated with the greatest tenderness. Anotah considered the doctress as her especial care, and watched over her like a mother.

X.

A Fresh Start.

Curtis and Ruth hardly knew whether they were regarded as prisoners or as guests by the Indians, with whom they were journeying. This point, however, was made clear as soon as the Indians had set up their white lodges, and enjoyed in them one comfortable night.

Ruth was roused from her morning sleep by Anotah's voice, and by the strong touch of the Indian girl's hand.

Anotah pointed to the east, which was already rosy with the light of the rising sun, and motioned to Ruth to follow her. Ruth obeyed as soon as possible.

She found Curtis already mounted upon Bob, and waiting, with Jerry saddled at his side.

John, meanwhile, was expressing his disapproval of the increase of several blankets and buffalo robes to his load, which the chief had presented to Curtis, with many signs of respect and kind interest.

The Indian encampment was only five miles from the emigrant road, but this fact the children did not know; and when the interpreter mounted a mule and prepared to lead the little party away from the Indian lodges, Ruth looked to Anotah for an explanation.

Could it be possible that they were to be taken into the pathless wilderness and left to find their own way, with only the stars as a guide?

Anotah quickly made the sign of a road along which people were passing, and closed with a bright smile, which said cheeringly, "Trust yourself to the guide; all will be well."

Ruth was surprised to find how hard it came to her to part with her Indian friend, and Anotah all at once made a similar discovery.

Ruth was on Jerry's back when Anotah came up to take her by the hand for the second time. As she did so Ruth's tears actually fell fast.

"Our Father, who art in heaven," repeated Ruth, slowly and distinctly, looking upward as she spoke.

Anotah folded her hands, repeating the words, "Our Father, who art in heaven."

Ruth pointed to the sun, and then to the east and the west, and gave an inquiring glance.

Anotah bowed towards the east and towards the west, signifying that she would use "Our Father" as a morning and an evening prayer.

"Good-bye," said Ruth, with an affectionate caress.

Anotah, quick as light, seized a horse which an Indian was holding near at hand. She mounted without a saddle, and thus intimated her intention to go with the party—for the present, at least.

How Ruth longed to be able to say some words which would fix Christian truth deep in Anotah's heart!

Silently the Indian girl rode at Ruth's side for the five long miles before they reached the emigrant road. Anotah's head frequently drooped upon her breast, and she seemed lost in thought.

Ruth, too, was silent. She was praying in her heart for the Indian tribes, and asking the Lord of heaven to raise up true-hearted Christian missionaries to labour among them.

The emigrant road was reached at last.

Anotah suddenly threw her scarlet blanket round Ruth, and then galloped away, her slender figure bare to the waist, and her head raised in the air, as though she were determined not to give way to sorrow.

The Indian guide swiftly followed, and Curtis and Ruth were once more alone on the beaten road.

Alone they were, but round them were strewn the never-failing signs of the great throng who had passed that way.

Anvils and shovels, cooking-stoves, carpenters'

tools, and empty trunks were strewn along the road, as if it were a market-day, and an invisible shopkeeper were offering his wares for sale to the passers-by.

Curtis was full of wonderful stories of his adventures among the Indians, while Ruth's loving heart was yearning over Anotah, and longing to know whether she was ever to be led into a belief in the only true God. Ruth was much refreshed by her stay among the Indians, and Curtis declared that he felt as if he were just starting on his journey.

In this spirit the children got on finely that day; and when they encamped at evening, they actually sat late at their fire, talking of the strange-looking rocks they had passed when with the Indians—"Chimney Rock" and the "Court House," as they have been called by travellers. Curtis and Ruth did not know them by these names, but Ruth declared that the sight of the tall bare rocks had been most welcome to her, they were so like the works of man. Ruth was beginning to long for human habitations again, and to think of Fort Laramie as a bright spot soon to be reached.

XI.

"This Philistine."

Curtis had never objected to resting on the Lord's-day, since he had bowed in the thunderstorm to ask forgiveness of his Maker. He felt the need of a day of rest, as well for his soul as his body. In the silence of a lonely encampment, God was particularly near to the children; and when their prayers and hymns rose on the clear air, there seemed to be nothing between them and the heaven towards which they were turning their thoughts.

This day Curtis had found a pleasant spot for their encampment, nearly a quarter of a mile from the road along which the tide of emigration flowed on all days of the week alike.

Ruth could not help thinking that the people who thus poured across the "Plains" from a Christian country, could not give the Indians a very favourable impression of the religion of their land. It was not only that the Sabbath was to them like other days, but they broke all the commandments as well as the fourth. Nor was this strange. They who disregard God's laws in one point, are sure, sooner or later, to show disrespect to all his requirements.

Ruth and Curtis were sitting in the shadow of a great rock, and talking cheerily of their mother, and the many sweet lessons she had taught them.

Their conversation was interrupted by the loud shouts of a party of emigrants, more rude and noisy than any they had seen. It was plain that they had been keeping up their sinking spirits by the fire-water, on which too many rely in their troubles.

"Do not let them see us!" said Ruth, slipping behind the rock so as to be out of sight.

Curtis thought it would be unmanly to withdraw from their observation, and so he kept his seat in full view of the noisy emigrants.

He soon started up, however, to hurry towards the long train of waggons.

Ruth called after him in vain. Curtis was drawn on by too strong a motive to be checked even by his sister's voice.

The mules had gradually wandered from the spot where Curtis and Ruth had stationed themselves, and had drawn near to the road.

To his great astonishment Curtis now saw them seized by several of the boisterous travellers, and driven in among their own animals, as if their rightful prey.

"They are ours!" shouted Curtis.

A laugh was the only reply.

"They are ours, and you *shall* give them up!" said Curtis angrily.

"*Shall!*" repeated half a dozen voices. "Shall!" and then followed a long, coarse laugh, that made Ruth feel as though she would gladly give up even the precious mules to be free from such bad company.

A shower of missiles was discharged at Curtis. Pans and pitchforks were thrown at him, and strong fists were clenched threateningly, as he was bidden to keep off, if he would save himself from hard usage.

Curtis saw that there was nothing to be gained from such a crew, but he resolved to try one expedient more. He gave a long, low whistle, which had hitherto succeeded in calling the mules to his side, no matter how far they had strayed from him.

Bob and Jerry were apparently too well pleased to be among companions of their own kind to obey the call, but John came jumping out of the drove, and with awkward gambols, threw up his heels, and deserted his new masters. Curtis came sadly back to Ruth, while John followed.

"We have only John now to depend upon! What is to become of us I cannot see. You certainly cannot ride him!" Curtis spoke disconsolately.

"Do you know what this rock makes me think of?" said Ruth, pointing to the wall of bare rock behind them.

"No!" said Curtis inquiringly.

"It reminds me of that sweet passage, 'He shall be like the shadow of a great rock in a weary land.' Curtis, we shall not be deserted. To-day we are comfortable. We did not intend to go on. We need no mules for our Sunday rest. We have our daily bread. We will not 'take thought for the morrow.'"

Some hard biscuit, which the Indians had procured from an emigrant train, had been Anotah's gift to Ruth; and now, with cold buffalo meat from the same source, the children made an excellent repast.

Ruth and Curtis had not only their faith to sustain them, but the natural joyousness of young hearts. The pleasant air, the sunshine, the birds, and the flowers, were all to them sources of pleasure. In that Sunday encampment they enjoyed the works of God, as well as put their trust in him for all their future lives.

XII.

Fort Laramie.

The day following, the young travellers had walked for at least eight miles, when they sat down wearied out, and glad to rest in the shade of a thick wood close upon the road.

They had hardly been seated five minutes when there was a roar near them that made the rocks ring, and it soon guided them to the spot where a fine cow was tossing her head in the air, as if calling for aid.

The creature seemed to understand at once that she had found a friend; and when Ruth's skilful hands began to make the milk flow, the wild bellowing was exchanged for such complacent mooing as children in the nursery like to imitate.

How refreshing that milk was to Curtis and Ruth! "This seems like real manna," said Ruth. "Who would have thought of our finding a cow here? Is it not wonderful, Curtis?"

"It is, indeed! I suppose she has strayed from some emigrant train. We will take her in charge until her owners claim her," said Curtis. "What shall we call her?"

"Suppose we call her Perdita. Don't you remember in our reading-book at school that was the name given to the lost child?" said Ruth.

"Yes, Perdita! That's capital. Do you suppose she'll follow us?" said Curtis.

When the sun had ceased to blaze down with noon-day heat, the children again started on their journey. They found no difficulty in persuading Perdita to be of their company. She seemed to understand that Ruth was her fast friend, and to look upon her with especial favour.

Curtis and Ruth had got on very comfortably for several days, travelling slowly, to be sure, but safe from the dangers of hunger and thirst, and cheered by the thought that they were drawing near Fort Laramie.

Perdita proved a perfect treasure. John's obstinacy was nearly subdued by the fatigues of the journey, and he was growing quite tractable.

On the fourth day after the loss of the other mules, Curtis was surprised to find John in a most excitable state. When he attempted to load him in the morning, he kicked violently, and plunged, as if in distress. His jaws were swollen, and Curtis fancied that his eyes looked strangely.

After much persuasion John was at length induced to receive the pack-saddle, and to set out for another day's work.

That was a weary day to the children. John failed hour by hour, and Curtis was at length sure that the mule had been bitten by a snake and would not survive the poisoned wound.

So, alas! it proved; before night-fall John had dropped dead by the road. Curtis sat down beside the poor creature's body, and said despondingly, "Now, Ruth, are you not ready to give up in despair?"

Ruth pointed at a rude substitute for a sign-board some passing emigrant had devised for the benefit of future travellers.

At a turn in the road stood a great tree, on whose brown trunk was carved, in immense letters, "Three Miles to Fort Laramie."

"Only three miles, Curtis! We can fancy we are driving Perdita home from pasture just towards evening, and go on that far very well. I know they will be kind to us at the fort."

Curtis wondered if any one could be unkind to Ruth. The answer came from his own conscience, and he felt ashamed to think how many times he had teased and worried her; and he resolved that if they were in a home again he would be very different from the "brother Curtis" of the Ohio farm.

The boy carried nothing of the mule's load but the blankets, that might be needed for the night should they fail to reach Fort Laramie.

Perdita's good milk would insure them a supper, and with this simple provision for the future, the children went forward.

There were several emigrant camps near Fort Laramie, but on the fort itself the children pressed. From the emigrants they might meet with rough treatment, but from the soldiers stationed in that far-off wilderness Ruth was sure of protection.

Ruth was not mistaken. Curtis had but to tell their sorrowful story, and point to Ruth, and the soldiers' hearts were at once moved to pity.

Again Ruth slept sweet sleep, and Curtis felt like a boy once more, relieved for the time from the burden of care that had oppressed him.

On awaking at Fort Laramie, Curtis began to consider what was to be done about the further prosecution of their journey. It was plain that he and Ruth must have an entirely new fitting out—Perdita, the blankets, and the tin cup being all their remaining valuables.

He was recommended to go to the emigrant camps, which were already in the bustle of starting.

Sellers were more plentiful than buyers in that region, and Curtis soon found himself in the midst of making bargains.

Ruth was forced to stay some days to recruit at Fort Laramie, and she was a most welcome visitor. The sight of her sweet young face was refreshing to the poor fellows, cut off from home ties and shut up there in the wilderness; Curtis, meanwhile, visited the various camps of travellers, and continued his purchases.

Ruth was alarmed lest he should spend all their money, merely for the pleasure of it. Curtis assured her that he was very judicious, though he did buy a hundred-weight of bacon, because he could get it for a cent (about a half-penny) a pound, when he had, as yet, no means of carrying it. Mules were scarce articles among the emigrants—at least mules in good condition—the burdens being more numerous than the beasts to carry them.

Every day Curtis learned more and more of the part of their journey still before them. Most discouraging were the accounts he received. He heard of portions of the route where there was not a bite of grass for the animals for a whole day's journey; and of others, where all the water was as salt as if it had been brought from the ocean itself.

Curtis told none of these tales to Ruth, who

was, as usual, giving no anxious thought to the future. She was faithfully doing the duty of the present hour, shedding the sunshine of cheerfulness around her, and diffusing the better light that made glad her own heart. Although she was forced to keep her blistered feet in a chair, her hands were constantly busy, and her needle was doing wonders in fitting up her brother's wardrobe and her own. Ruth had learned by experience what materials were best for clothing for the journey she had before her, and the German woman's valuables proved of the right sort.

"You don't mean to start off alone again with that sister of yours!" said a soldier to Curtis.

Curtis was bargaining for a mule, and at first he pretended not to hear the remark. The bargain was concluded, and Curtis had changed Perdita for a strong-limbed animal, declared to be in famous order for travelling.

"I say," pressed the same soldier, "do you mean to start off that little pale-faced thing across the desert ahead, with only you to look out for her? If you do, you deserve nothing better than to have the Pawnees get your scalp."

Curtis had already had misgivings about undertaking the rest of the journey in the same unprotected way in which they had hitherto travelled. He felt more pride than he would have confessed in having thus far been his sister's sole guardian, and he did not at all relish the idea of giving up a triumph when it was half won.

The adventurous boy had no time for further thought just then, for a band of men at that moment came in sight. They moved slowly, and it was soon plain that they were bringing wounded soldiers to the fort.

"They've had a brush with the Indians. I wonder who is hurt!" said the soldier, hastening away to hear the news.

Ruth had been thinking that the men at Fort Laramie led a lazy life, and that after all it was not unpleasant to step about to the sound of music, go through military drilling, and be called a soldier. Her opinion changed suddenly as she caught sight of the wounded, bleeding men, who were borne to the hospital tent. Her heart yearned to go and wait upon them; but her proposal to do so was received with a laugh, and the answer, "They are used to rough nursing. You would faint even to see the poor fellows' ghastly wounds."

The road from Fort Laramie to Fort Bridger was said to be infested with bands of Indians, who had lately been very troublesome to the emigrants, and had killed outright two small parties whom they surprised in a lonely place.

All this made but a slight impression upon Ruth, as far as personal danger was concerned.

She looked upon the continuation of their journey as a necessary evil for her brother and herself, and trusted that they would be watched over in the future as they had been in the past. Of emigrant parties Ruth had a perfect horror. She had seen enough of them to feel that the evil which prevailed among them was more to be dreaded than the worst dangers of the road. One point Ruth had settled in her own mind—she would not connect herself with any of those Sabbath-breaking, unprincipled parties.

Curtis, meanwhile, was coming to a different conclusion, and was on the watch for such a train as it would be advisable to join. He loved Ruth too well needlessly to expose her to the danger of another trip, such as they had had since they left Fort Kearney.

He was told there was not a single human habitation from Fort Laramie to Fort Bridger, a distance of four hundred miles. He would not venture upon a journey through that dangerous region without some safeguard. So he plainly told Ruth, and made her understand that she must submit to his will.

"You are very uncharitable, Ruth, to suppose that among all the crowds of people crossing the 'Plains' from the States there are no true Christians! Have not the people who meet us a right to judge us in the same way?" Curtis had now good sense on his side, and Ruth felt it as she answered—

"I am afraid I am like the prophet who thought he only was left to serve the true God, when the Lord had reserved for himself seven thousand men who had not bowed the knee to Baal."

"We shall see," said Curtis. "We shall see."

Evening was coming on, and several emigrant trains pitched their camps in the neighbourhood of Fort Laramie. To these Curtis made his way, with a prayer on his lips that he might be guided to companions suitable and profitable for himself and his loving sister.

He had learned to *pray;* he had learned to ask for what he needed—to ask for his " daily bread " as well as " deliverance from evil."

His search for a while seemed vain. There was the same boisterous roughness in the first two camps he visited, as he had seen by the way. He would not place Ruth among such associates. " No, not for the world!"

More distant from Fort Laramie than the encampments already mentioned, a cluster of white waggons had been arranged for the night. As Curtis drew near them, a most welcome sound saluted his ears. An evening hymn rose on the air. Curtis, almost from habit, joined in the familiar words,—

" Rock of Ages, cleft for me,
Let me hide myself in thee!"

CURTIS AND THE CAPTAIN.
Page 93.

"Here surely must be friends," said Curtis to himself as he made his way into the midst of the encampment. A tall, sunburnt man came forward to receive him, and inquire his business.

"I did come on business," said Curtis in a manly way, "but first I want to shake hands with all who sang that hymn. It is a good thing to hear that kind of singing in this heathen land."

"Then shake the captain's hand, for he proposed it," said several voices.

The tall stranger who had first addressed Curtis extended a brown, hard hand, marked with many a scar. After a hearty greeting, Curtis told his business. He wanted to connect himself with a respectable party going westward —a party where intemperance, and profanity, and wickedness generally, were not countenanced. He wanted to place his dear little sister under the care of some motherly woman, who would watch over her, and feel a kind interest in her. He wished to pay for a safe escort, and also to provide his share of the provisions consumed by the way. He remembered the lot of cheap bacon.

Curtis was allowed to finish all he had to say without interruption; then the person called the captain replied.

Captain G—— was an old *voyageur*, one who had lived west of Missouri for many, many years, and was more at home on the "Plains" than in the midst of the dwellings of civilized man. Much hard fighting and many perilous hunts he had seen. As the brook followed the Israelites through the wilderness, one pure stream had been with the hardy man in all his wanderings, even the remembrance of the pious teachings of his mother. Often, he said, by the lonely camp-fire, he had recalled her sweet voice, as she had taught him to sing of Jesus, or offer prayer in his powerful, all-prevailing name.

Such remembrances had lingered with Captain G——, but he had "gone far astray, and erred like a lost sheep."

Acting as a guide to travellers and emigrant parties, he had become like the roughest among them. Once, however, it was his privilege to be the head of a company who had among them an earnest missionary, bound for a station on the shores of the Pacific. He would ever have reason to bless that journey and that missionary.

Through the mercy of God, and the faithful efforts of the Christian traveller, Captain G——'s course was for ever changed. He no longer merely cherished a sweet memory of his mother's teachings, but strove to walk in the way in which he had been trained as a child.

He devoted himself to God in the same calling he had so long followed. He would be a guide and a leader to emigrant parties; and while he piloted them across the dreary "Plains," strive to point them to the heavenly country, stored with better treasure than the gold of California.

Such was the person to whom Curtis had been led. He could not doubt that the providential Hand had been with him, and so said Captain G——.

Freely Curtis was welcomed to the party, and Captain G—— declared that he longed to have little Ruth under his special protection. Before they parted it was arranged that the children should move with the camp at daybreak on the morrow.

XIII.

𝔐rs. 𝔑utten.

Curtis had not seen the "motherly person" to whose charge Ruth was to be particularly confided, on the journey from Fort Laramie to Fort Bridger. Of course he had fancied somebody resembling his own lost mother, and possessed of all the womanly charms of woman in civilized life. Both Ruth and her brother were not a little surprised, therefore, at the face that looked out from the waggon, which was to be Ruth's temporary home.

"Here! put her in here!" cried a loud, coarse voice, that made the observer look twice to see that the speaker was not a man.

"You see Mrs. Nutten is quite ready for you, Ruth," said Captain G——, as he helped the little girl into the waggon.

"All trig, girl, and just room enough left for you there, with your back to the feather bed," said Mrs. Nutten, putting Ruth in the place, much as a child would a doll in a baby-house.

Curtis gave a glance at Ruth, to see how she liked the appearance of her new companion.

Ruth returned one of her sweet smiles, which reassured the brother's heart.

"I'll stand here, by you, till we start," said Curtis. "Now, Ruthy, you look so well, a great deal better—I mean, more healthy than you did when we got here—"

What more Curtis might have said we cannot tell, for at that moment Captain G—— called him away to unpack his mule, which, the old guide said, was about as badly laden as it could be.

Curtis soon found that Captain G—— well deserved his title, though he had never served in the regular army, or even in a raw militia company. He was evidently born to command, and made sure of the good of his party by keeping them all strictly obedient to orders. Mutineers or rebels against his authority were to be dropped by the way, and left to shift for themselves; that was one of the captain's regulations, made known to every individual before he started one step on the journey.

Curtis was not inclined to mutiny; he was pleased with the rough captain, and deeply thankful to have secured the escort of one so skilled in the ways of the wilderness.

Ruth was startled to see the emigrants all called to stand before Captain G—— before setting out, that he might examine the various rifles and muskets with which they were armed.

"You won't kill anybody, if you can help it?" Ruth ventured to say to the captain, as he passed near her.

"Indeed we won't! We must be on the safe side, though. I always see that these arguments are in order; but then, I try all soft means with our red brothers first. Sometimes nothing will quiet them but the bullets."

Ruth drew back into the waggon, not to dwell with terror on the possible skirmishes of the way, but to pray, in her own simple, but fervent manner, that the time might soon come when wars should cease, and red men and white men both love and honour the same Lord.

The long train was at length ready to start, and then to Ruth's surprise, all broke forth into the cheerful hymn,—

"I am bound for the land of Canaan."

Rising over all the other voices, were heard the captain's strong tones, while Mrs. Nutten seemed doing her best to rival him.

"Do you ride easy?" said Mrs. Nutten, kindly, to Ruth, as soon as the singing was over. "Do you ride easy, dear?"

"I am very comfortable," replied Ruth, with a grateful smile.

"I greased the wheels well at the fort, and she's a staunch old creature. I don't doubt she'll stand it to the end," complacently rejoined Mrs. Nutten.

Ruth looked doubtfully about her, to see the feminine being referred to. She soon learned that Mrs. Nutten had, for lack of another companion, fallen into the way of talking to her waggon, and fancying it had as much feeling and individuality as herself. She evidently loved the great lumbering vehicle as the sailor does his ship.

Mrs. Nutten favoured Ruth, from time to time, with various snatches of her history. The young traveller soon learned that her companion was going to California to meet one Philip Nutten, whom she had sent out to get things ready there, while she settled up matters in Indiana, and got all straight for the move. This "getting all straight" turned out to be the sale of the valuables belonging to the Nutten family, with the exception of a few necessaries for the way,—the never-to-be-despised waggon, and its adjuncts, the mules. Philip Nutten was of course the husband of the vigorous traveller—a person for whom she seemed to have a strong attachment, though it was evident that she considered it a mercy to him to be connected with a person so capable of advising him, and taking the general care of him.

"What would Philip Nutten say to this?"

exclaimed the good woman. "What a waste! What a waste!"

Such exclamations as these were frequent with Mrs. Nutten, as she passed the various articles of property strewed along the emigrant road. Ploughs lay in a soil too dry and barren to produce a breakfast for a weary mule. Carpenters' tools were dropped where not a tree, or a shrub, but the stunted artemisia, was to be seen for many a weary mile. Bonnets and band-boxes, trunks and pitchers, sprinkled the ground, until Mrs. Nutten was wrought up to a great pitch of indignation, that people should choose to "waste good money buying things to be just thrown away, for *Injins* to pick up and buffaloes to tread on!"

Ruth was surprised to find how comfortably she was making this difficult part of the journey. Mrs. Nutten was evidently a capital manager; and although she had, as she said, "never been bothered with any children of her own," it was plain that the presence of Ruth was by no means disagreeable to her.

Day by day Ruth learned that Mrs. Nutten spoke ill of no *individuals*, though she was very severe on certain *classes* of "shiftless folks and ne'er-do-wells," on whom she frequently vented her wrath in the severest terms.

Mrs. Nutten was always willing to help a

fellow-emigrant at a camping-ground; and at every step was sure to look after a certain "young thing with a baby," who seemed, of all the party, to have her particular interest.

Yes, Mrs. Nutten, rough and queer as she was, had a kind, true heart. Captain G—— knew that, or he would not have placed the little pale-faced Ruth under her charge. He knew the delicate girl would be better off there than in the great waggon, where Curtis had found a place with him.

Curtis felt it quite an honour to have a position with the captain, and thought he was daily growing wonderfully wise in hunter's craft, and expedients for safe and easy travelling on the "Plains."

All this wisdom Curtis was willing to have in theory for the present. He only realized how much he had suffered in trying to be a man, by finding out how delightful it was to be a boy again at Captain G——'s side, listening to his adventures, and following his directions, sure that they were wisely given.

Curtis did not wonder at the influence Captain G—— had in his party. He soon found out that the captain's strength of character was equalled by his sincerity and earnestness as a Christian. He would wink at no wrong-doing, countenance no evil ways in his company. He said he had asked the blessing of God on that emigrant train, and God's ten commandments he would see enforced.

"I wonder how Mrs. Nutten came to join this party, not being a Christian woman," said Curtis to Ruth some days after they left Fort Laramie.

"Not a Christian woman!" said Ruth in surprise. "How mistaken you are, brother! I do not believe she would do a thing she knew to be wrong, if she were to be tempted with waggon loads of gold. She's rough, but she's true, Curtis. I have learned something. All good people are not alike; and they are not all gentle and soft-spoken like mother."

"And like you too, Ruth. The captain says, —well, don't redden up so rosy. I won't tell you what he says. But, Ruthy, we will never say *all* emigrants are bad again, will we?"

"No, Curtis, I never mean to judge hardly of any kind of people again," said Ruth, earnestly. "Why, I really love Mrs. Nutten. She is as kind as she can be."

"And she'll love you, I know, Ruth. Everybody does, and no wonder," said Curtis, warmly.

Yes, Ruth's loving spirit was sure to make friends for her everywhere. As there are sunshine and dew for the flowers, so love and kindness will always spring up for the gentle and unselfish.

XIV.
Westward.

Five days after Captain G——'s train left Fort Laramie, they came to the point where Deer Creek flows into the Platte. Near this spot there was a wide ferry, by which emigrants were enabled to cross the river in safety. Swimming it had proved a fatal experiment to many travellers, and Captain G—— wisely resolved to avail himself of the ferry for his party. Seven trunks of cotton-wood trees had been hewn out into canoes, and these canoes, fastened together by strong cross-poles, formed the rude raft to which the travellers were to intrust their safety. When it came Mrs. Nutten's turn to be pulled across, she set the mules at liberty, and saw them swim to the other side.

"I am afraid *she'll* sink!" said Mrs. Nutten, with a doubtful look.

"She aint heavy enough to weigh down a walnut shell!" exclaimed one of the ferrymen, laughing, as he looked at Ruth, supposing her to be the precious cargo about whom the good woman was so anxious.

"Pshaw! the waggon, I mean. Do you think *she'll* go over safe?" said Mrs. Nutten.

"Only try *her!*" said the ferryman, putting the waggon on to the raft. "*She's* a beauty!"

In a few moments the whole affair was drawn across the stream by the rope, which was attached to a huge tree on the other side.

"*She's* sound!" said Mrs. Nutten, looking at her treasure in triumph, as it was landed on the opposite bank. Without a murmur she paid the two dollars charged for the ferriage, declaring the money was well spent.

Ruth thought of the waggon she and Curtis had left in the water, far, far, back, when they had first crossed the Platte. What an age it seemed to her since that time!

Now she was soon to bid good-bye to the river. Soon it would take its sudden southern bend, while the emigrant road would keep steadily on to the west. Up to this point the route of the children from Fort Kearney can be very nearly traced by looking on the map of the United States, at the course of the North Fork of the Platte, and of the main river from that point.

After leaving the Platte, the road lay along the Sweetwater, until it nearly reached the South Pass.

Yes, Curtis and Ruth crossed the Rocky Mountains at this point, and would not have known that they were going through this far-famed opening in the range, if Captain G—— had not ordered a halt while he announced the good news to the whole party.

"The streams from this point all flow west, and find their way into the old Pacific," said Captain G——. "We've passed the turning-point. We'll ask the blessing of God on our trip this side of the mountains."

The captain's strong voice made the words of prayer heard along the line, and his loud "Amen!" was responded to with heartiness as earnest as that with which it was spoken.

"To be west of the Rocky Mountains! How strange that seems!" said Ruth to Mrs. Nutten.

"It seems good! Why, every bit of running water going west makes me feel that I am getting towards Philip Nutten. How does he get along without me?"

The good woman seemed half ashamed of her affection for her husband, who, it had transpired, was half a head shorter than herself, and the younger of the two by ten years.

If Philip Nutten were a delicate man, he certainly had secured a good nurse, rough though she was in some of her ways.

It was three weeks from the time their train left Fort Laramie before it reached the South Pass, and in that time Mrs. Nutten had found various ways of making the fatigues and annoyances of the journey tolerable to Ruth.

When the hot air blistered Ruth's face, and the drifting sand almost blinded her eyes, Mrs. Nutten clipped out a cloth mask for her face, and covered her eyes with a bit of oil-silk she had in her capacious pocket.

For Ruth she secured the choicest bits of the game killed on the road. For Ruth she was sure to get a draught of fresh water as soon as the train reached a spring or a running stream.

Streams and springs had both been rare on the journey, and the whole party had suffered much from thirst. But when Ruth reached Fort Bridger she felt less exhausted than at her previous stoppages at Fort Laramie and Fort Kearney. Mrs. Nutten had been a kind, devoted friend to Ruth. Captain G—— had well understood how to guide and regulate his party.

"We could not have made this part of the journey alone," said Curtis to Ruth, when they were safely encamped near Fort Bridger.

"No; indeed we could not!" was the reply. "What a kind Providence it was that gave us such friends in our time of need!"

To Ruth all gifts, all blessings, all friends were but reminders of the continual presence of the great heavenly Friend in whom she put her trust. He truly is "about our path and our lying down, and knoweth all our ways."

XV.

Salt Lake City.

Fort Bridger is an Indian trading-post, owned by Major James Bridger, whose kind hospitality so many western travellers have shared. Captain G—— was well known at Fort Bridger, and there easily obtained permission to have the waggons of his train thoroughly repaired, and his mules carefully shod. When this was done the captain declared that he saw no reason for further delay, as every day was now precious. Autumn, he said, would fairly set in before the party reached California, and there must be no " dilly-dallying " by the way. Our emigrant party had the usual share of discomfort and fatigue in the two weeks that it took them to proceed from Fort Bridger to Salt Lake City. They had no special adventure worthy of record, save the meeting of occasional bands of Snake Indians, or root-diggers—miserable, half-clad creatures, who live more like wild beasts than human beings. Mrs. Nutten was much shocked at their appearance and manners, and declared her intention of establishing a sewing society for their benefit as soon as she reached California, a promise which she literally kept, though Philip Nutten was the only person who responded to her call to assist in this charity.

"Philip could handle his needle right well," Mrs. Nutten said; "and why should he not, as he had been born and bred a tailor?"

Mrs. Nutten was talking, as usual, of Philip and her views respecting him, when the emigrant party came in sight of Salt Lake City.

"The Mormon Babylon!" exclaimed Mrs. Nutten. "I wouldn't set foot in it if you were to pay me for it!"

Mrs. Nutten was true to her word. Curiosity could not tempt her to hold any communication with people who, as she said, "put by the Testament, and followed after that hypocritical Joe Smith! Other folks might do as they pleased, but Philip Nutten's wife would keep clear of Mormons as she would of snakes."

Salt Lake City was not a very grand affair, and yet it was a wonderfully large settlement to be flourishing there in the wilderness. The poor, misguided people who had clustered in the Great Salt Lake Basin were objects of strong interest to Ruth. When Captain G—— told her that one unfortunate woman, who had been led away by the Mormons, had begged to join his train, and go back to live among Christians, Ruth rejoiced from the bottom of her heart.

Curtis was full of interest about the Great Salt Lake, and highly enjoyed a trip to its borders which he took with Captain G——. He was surprised to find its banks bleak and bare, while a heavy mist hung over the moist plains about it. Great rocky islands towered from its midst, and flocks of pigeons and swans sported upon its waters; yet Curtis turned away from it with a feeling of desolation and loneliness. It seemed so like the Dead Sea, where Sodom and Gomorrah lie buried for ever.

We will not trace the passage of our travellers from Salt Lake City to California, now that they are under good guidance. Ruth had become stronger and stronger every day since Mrs. Nutten had taken her under her charge, and at length the good woman declared, if Ruth's hands were only large enough, she might be trusted to drive the six mules, she had such muscle in her arms!

This was somewhat of an exaggeration; and, be it observed, Mrs. Nutten never for a moment trusted Ruth with *her* safety—her meaning the waggon, of course.

Ruth, meanwhile, thought little of the dangers or incidents of the way, and, it must be owned, she lost many of the anecdotes of Philip Nutten with which her companion favoured her ear. Ruth had an absorbing subject of thought: How and where would she find her father? Was he yet living? Was he like the rough, unprincipled emigrants whom she had seen on the "Plains?"

Curtis, too, was much harassed by thoughts of the same kind. The more truly he became himself a Christian, the more he trembled for his father's present condition. His remembrances of that father were by no means encouraging. A wild, reckless man, more fond of merry-making than of labour, Curtis was sure that he had been, even among the restraints of civilized society, and with the safeguard of a loving, true-hearted wife. What had he become amid the temptations of California?

Whatever that father might be, Curtis resolved to be to him a dutiful, affectionate son. The humbled boy felt in his own heart a but half-subdued waywardness, that made him realize that his own course might have ended in shame, but for the mercy of God, which had roused his soul to better things. That mercy might yet reach his father—for this Ruth and Curtis prayed day by day.

Curtis had ascertained that many of the emigrants in Captain G——'s party were to stop at some of the most eastern settlements in California, while Ruth and himself were bound to San Francisco.

Captain G—— avowed his intention of accompanying the children to their journey's end. The good man, in his heart, doubted much whether they would find their father, and had resolved to be himself a father to them should they be left orphans.

Mrs. Nutten grew uncommonly tender towards Ruth, as they neared the confines of California, and was actually heard to say, that she had often advised Philip Nutten to adopt a child, and if he did, she wouldn't mind taking Ruth, for better or for worse.

As Mrs Nutten's beloved vehicle was entering a small California village one evening in September, suddenly the tall woman tossed the reins into Ruth's hands, and, leaping from the waggon, she threw her arms round the neck of a short man, who was looking earnestly from waggon to waggon along the train.

"Philip! Philip Nutten!" exclaimed the wife, as she fairly lifted the little fellow off his feet in her joy at the re-union.

"Betsy Nutten! my Betsy!" was all that Philip found words to say.

"How came you here? I didn't say settle here!" said Betsy, when her first astonishment was over.

"I didn't set up here; I just came out from San Francisco, hoping to meet you," was Philip's humble reply.

A general introducing now took place, and then Mrs. Nutten announced to Philip that she had to go "a piece" further without him, until she dropped her passenger; and so they parted, not, however, without an agreement being made for their future meeting. Mrs. Nutten, like Captain G——, thought it very probable that Mr. Sumner would be either no longer living, or an unfit person to have the charge of the delicate Ruth. Betsy Nutten had no idea, she said, of giving up Ruth, unless she was going to fall into proper hands.

The other waggons dropped away, one by one, but Captain G——'s and Mrs. Nutten's still held on towards San Francisco.

XVI.

Realities.

After much hunting up and down the streets of San Francisco, the obscure lodging-house was pointed out where Thomas Sumner was to be found.

Captain G—— shook his head, and exchanged glances with Mrs. Nutten, as they made application at the house.

"He not see anybody; he sick," was the answer made by the Chinese servant who opened the door.

"Which way? which way?" said Ruth, hurrying into the narrow entry.

"Show his room directly," said Curtis, with an air of command.

In a back room on the lower floor Ruth found her father. Her worst fears were realized. No, not her *worst* fears, for while there is life there is hope.

Thomas Sumner had run through a wild career of extravagance and dissipation, and now, prostrate in body and distressed in mind, he lay moaning on a bed of sickness.

"Father! dear father!" said Ruth, drawing near to the bedside.

The sick man turned suddenly, as if heavenly music had struck upon his ears.

"We have come to take care of you," said Curtis, in a tone hoarse with deep feeling.

"Your mother?" said the poor man, with a wild, questioning glance.

"She died before we reached Fort Leavenworth," said Curtis. "We had no one left but you, and so we came on. Ruth, too, had a message for you."

"Yes, mother said she hoped to meet you in heaven, father. She looked so full of joy and peace when she said that!"

The poor man groaned, and turned his face to the wall. What right had he to the loving care of such children?—the children of his Mary!

Captain G—— and Mrs. Nutten had fully determined to take Ruth and Curtis under their charge, if their father should prove unworthy; but how could they deny the sick, perhaps dying man the angels of mercy which a providential Hand had sent to him in his hour of need? They would rather stay and join the children in their labour of love.

Ruth was repaid for all the pains and weariness of the journey when she found at what a welcome moment she had arrived. She was wanted, truly, to minister to her father's sick soul as well as to his suffering body. Love and self-sacrifice will touch the most hardened heart.

When Thomas Sumner heard how his little Ruth had bravely borne all things that she might bring to him his wife's dying message, he was touched and softened.

So the way was made open for better things. He saw and felt his own fearful unworthiness. Then it was Ruth's precious privilege to speak to him of the blessed Saviour, who welcomes the returning prodigal, and loves them for whom he willingly offered himself an atoning sacrifice.

Thomas Sumner listened, believed, and rejoiced.

And Ruth! They only can understand her feelings who have had their fervent prayers for dearest friends thus granted by the unutterable goodness of a merciful Redeemer.

XVII.

Home.

Ten years have passed since Curtis and Ruth Sumner made their overland journey to California.

Curtis is a man now, full six feet in his stockings—a sturdy, healthy, happy *Ohio* farmer.

An Ohio farmer? Yes, he has bought back the old place, where the honeysuckle still grows over the pantry windows—where his mother lived! Money-making is not his object in life; he has another and a better motive. And yet the farm is larger than it was in the old days, and Thomas Sumner says it was never in so fine a condition. Thomas Sumner misses the face that used to greet him at the threshold; he misses the sweet voice at the fireside. His Mary is no more on earth, to bear patiently with his follies, and gently give him sweet counsel. He feels that he did not deserve her, and he bows to the stroke. Yet he loves the spot hallowed by her memory. He cannot blot out the past; that is not in the power of any human being. The wrong actions, the harsh words, of days gone by, must do their work. The sinner is forgiven, but the sin has to go on with its mischief till the end of time, for "one sinner destroyeth much good." Thomas Sumner knows that. He remembers the baneful influence he has formerly exercised, and with deep humility owns that he is unworthy, utterly unworthy, of his many blessings. He feels that he does not deserve his dear, dutiful children. From the depths of his heart he daily says, "I have erred, and strayed from thy ways like a lost sheep;" but he remembers the words of the Saviour, who came to "seek and to save that which is lost," and he is comforted.

Curtis ever treats his father with kindness and respect; yet Thomas Sumner feels humbled when he looks his noble son in the face. He half fancies, too, that Curtis, in his heart, cannot reverence and love him.

There is one human being upon whom Thomas Sumner ever looks without dropping his eyes in shame. He knows that Ruth's love has blotted out the remembrance of his transgressions. He knows that to her he is the dear father whom she perilled her life to save—the dear father whom she rejoices to see walking in the ways of holiness. He can kneel at Ruth's side, and confess his sins in brokenness of heart, and know she loves him the better for his true penitence.

Dear Ruth, hers is a happy lot. She has the blessing for which she cares the most. Her two dear ones are true servants of God—safe in his covenant-keeping. Her days flow by in pleasant home-cares. She loves to hear Curtis say that she constantly grows more like her mother; and when her father's eye rests upon her, it speaks a blessing.

Thomas Sumner is not a poor man now. The industry of father and son was successful in California. They have more than enough for their own comfort. Ruth knows how to use the surplus. She does not forget the heathen in foreign lands. She clothes the poor, who are scattered in her own neighbourhood. She has her Sunday school class,—a happy little group, that gather round her, looking up to her for spiritual food, like nestlings to the mother-bird.

Ruth has many calls upon her time and purse, but one object is dearer to her than all the others; one appeal seems ever present in her heart: she has not forgotten the heathen at home. She remembers the destitute places of the West. She remembers the Christless multitudes she saw on the "Plains,"—Indians and white men, alike forgetful of God. Ah! how she loves to help the missionaries who are labouring among them! how she loves to send good books where the living preacher cannot go! Ruth's heart is in that work. She sanctifies it with her prayers, and God's blessing goes with her efforts.

XVIII.

Conclusion.

RUTH is social in her nature. She is given to hospitality. Not that she is in favour of great merry-makings and country frolics, but she loves to have others occasionally enjoy a happy home.

Last Christmas she had a guest that it was joy to her to entertain. A tall, dark man, he was not a beauty; and yet Ruth looked at him as if she reverenced his iron-grey looks, and loved his weather-worn features.

It was plain that the stranger was a favourite with Curtis too. Though not over-fond of late sittings at the fire, Curtis had twice been up until midnight, listening to the visitor's stories—stories of wild buffalo-hunts, and escapes among the Indians.

Of course it was Captain G——, the dear old captain, who had come to Ohio on purpose to see "his children," as he called the tall, sturdy Curtis, and the delicate, graceful, womanly Ruth. His "children" he had a right to call them, for he loved them with almost a father's love, and he had given them more than a father's care during their first year in California.

Now he rejoiced in their tranquil prosperity, and he wanted to see it with his own eyes.

He had news, moreover—news for Ruth, a message from her friend, Mrs. Nutten. Mrs. Nutten had now a flourishing hotel in California,—a hotel where there was no bar, and no gambling—an orderly, home-like place—where young men might be safe from temptation, and share her motherly care with Philip Nutten. Philip had used his needle and shears to advantage, and ventured to have his own name on his shining new sign, without so much as saying that he was husband to Betsy Nutten! The world knew it, though; so he had the honour, without boasting of it publicly. All this the captain told Curtis and Ruth, of course, and they laughed as they listened.

"Betsy said: 'Tell Ruth I love her clear down in my heart, and when I am on my knees I always think of her. She's kinder fast right on to the best part of my spirit. I've got something for her, too. I am going to send her a real valuable present.'"

"Of course," continued the captain, "I expected to have a jar of sweetmeats, or some such nonsense, to be bothered with; but Betsy took out this little Bible from her pocket. 'Give this to Ruth,' says she. 'Tell her one Collot, a French trader, left it at my hotel. He kept it under his pillow till he died—and he died calling on the name of Jesus. He was a thorough Christian, that man, for all the wild life he had led. That little Bible was by him to the last. He never trusted it in anybody's hand while he was living; but when he was gone I dared to open it. There was the name, on the title page—Ruth Sumner. Then I knew the dear child had been scattering the good seed, and God had blessed it—thanks be unto his name!'"

Ruth fairly sobbed as the captain finished his story.

"God has blessed *her*, thanks be unto his name!" said Thomas Sumner, solemnly.

Captain G—— broke forth into a hymn of praise, in which the whole family joined.

Yes, praised be His holy name, who "willeth not the death of a sinner!" He prospers our efforts in his cause! We have but to persevere, and scatter the good seed, and the Lord of the harvest will crown the work of our hands with abundant success.

www.ingramcontent.com/pod-product-compliance
Lightning Source LLC
Chambersburg PA
CBHW020120170426
43199CB00009B/571